D0923930

Online by Design

Online by Design

The Essentials of Creating Information Literacy Courses

Yvonne Mery and Jill Newby

ROWMAN & LITTLEFIELD
Lanham • Boulder • New York • Toronto • Plymouth, UK

Published by Rowman & Littlefield
4501 Forbes Boulevard, Suite 200, Lanham, Maryland 20706
www.rowman.com

10 Thornbury Road, Plymouth PL6 7PP, United Kingdom

Copyright © 2014 by Rowman & Littlefield

All rights reserved. No part of this book may be reproduced in any form or by any electronic or mechanical means, including information storage and retrieval systems, without written permission from the publisher, except by a reviewer who may quote passages in a review.

British Library Cataloguing in Publication Information Available

Library of Congress Cataloging-in-Publication Data

Mery, Yvonne.
  Online by design : the essentials of creating information literacy courses / Yvonne Mery and Jill Newby.
    pages cm.
  Includes index.
  ISBN 978-0-8108-9111-1 (pbk. : alk. paper) — ISBN 978-0-8108-9112-8 (electronic)
  1. Information literacy—Web-based instruction. 2. Web-based instruction—Design.
  3. Web-based instruction—Evaluation. I. Newby, Jill. II. Title.
  ZA3075.M47 2014
  028.70285—dc23   2013050182

∞™ The paper used in this publication meets the minimum requirements of American National Standard for Information Sciences—Permanence of Paper for Printed Library Materials, ANSI/NISO Z39.48-1992.

Printed in the United States of America

DEDICATION

For Chiara who has made me laugh each and every day, even before I met her.

In memory of Patricia Promis, who introduced me to the wonderful world of libraries.

To Dan Lee for his patience and support always, and my father, for among other things, being a great teacher.

Contents

List of Figures   ix

List of Tables   xi

Foreword   xiii

Preface   xv

Acknowledgments   xix

1   Introduction   1

SECTION 1: DEVELOPING THE COURSE

2   The Nuts and Bolts of Online Credit Courses: What You Need to Know before You Start   13

3   A Recipe for Success: Cooking up the Curriculum   29

4   Creating a Student-Centered Syllabus: Taking It to the Next Level   49

SECTION 2: DEVELOPING THE UNITS

5   Learning Materials 101: Variety Is the Spice of Life   79

6   Tutorials 101: Keeping Students Engaged   103

7   Assignments 101: Making It Real, Related, and Rewarding   121

8   But Did They Learn Anything? Assessing and Evaluating   143

9   New Models for Teaching and Learning   169

Index   175

About the Authors   179

Figures

2.1 Marketing Materials for an Undergraduate Course   24

2.2 Marketing Materials for a Graduate Course   24

4.1 Interactive Syllabus for an Information Literacy Course 57

4.2 Interactive Syllabus for an Emerging Media Course   58

5.1 Default Course Home Page   93

5.2 Custom Home Page with Clear Navigation   94

5.3 Course Content Page with Unit Outcomes and Other Links   95

6.1 Tutorial with Application of Skills as a Drag and Drop   108

6.2 Interactive Guide on the Side Tutorial   111

6.3 Tutorial with Both Redundant Text and Spoken Narration 113

6.4 Tutorial with Gratuitous Decorative Image   114

6.5 Tutorial with Ineffective Use of Labeling   114

6.6 Tutorial with More Effective Use of Labeling   115

8.1 Multiple-Choice Test Item Terminology   147

8.2 Analytic Rubric—Open Access Publishing Assignment   153

8.3 Holistic Rubric—Research Portfolio Assignment   154

Tables

3.1 Passive and Active Learning Outcomes   38

3.2 Outcomes Aligned with Bloom's Taxonomy   40

3.3 Bloom's Taxonomy and Action Verbs   40

6.1 Active and Passive Learning   105

8.1 Multiple-Choice Items Aligned with Bloom's Taxonomy   147

Foreword

Online instruction is about, first and foremost, student learning. Although this may seem obvious, it is not uncommon for this crucial point to get overshadowed by the trendiness of new technologies. For a variety of reasons, online education will continue to grow, making it increasingly important for librarians to understand how to create engaging materials and teach effectively in this medium. Fortunately, Mery and Newby, the authors of *Online by Design: The Essentials of Creating Information Literacy Courses*, have shared their rich experiences with online course development through this volume.

For a library course to be successful, those developing the course must have a sound pedagogical foundation, knowledge of instructional technologies, and a willingness to approach teaching online as an opportunity to increase student engagement and enhance learning. The authors use recent research studies to bring the latest evidence of good practice to the readers' attention and provide engaging pedagogical practices for a variety of formats that all instruction librarians can adopt in their own instructional activities.

This book is timely for those in the initial stages of creating an online course or contemplating the conversion of a face-to-face course to an online format. It is well written and organized; because each chapter can stand on its own, this is also a useful guide for those beginning the foray into the online environment with smaller activities such as the integration of content into an existing disciplinary course or the assessment of an instructional module. This book is a welcome addition to librarians' professional development toolkits.

Karen Williams

Preface

When Yvonne, one of the authors, was in grade school, students were told that in the future teachers would be replaced by computers. In typical third-grade fashion, she pictured a regular classroom with students in rows at their desks and a computer at the front of the class where the teacher once stood. Students would interact with one another and with the robotic teacher at the front of the class. Fast forward some thirty years and Yvonne found herself completing her graduate studies in library science in much the same way she had envisioned it at the tender age of eight. Of course, there were some differences: The classroom was actually the nearest coffeehouse; students were scattered across the globe; and the teacher was a professor halfway across the state. With some of these graduate courses she felt as though she was in the type of classroom she had envisioned so many years ago with students at the next desk and a professor at the head of the class. Other courses felt like an experiment in extreme isolation with nowhere to go for help.

What distinguished these good courses from the bad ones? How do we maximize the good and limit the bad? How can we ensure that our students feel connected with one another? These are a few of the many questions that we asked ourselves when we were assigned the task of developing our library's first online courses. Unfortunately, we had few resources to guide us. Online courses were still (and perhaps are still) in their infancy and were not as commonplace on college campuses as they are today. In addition, little had been written on online information literacy specific courses. Now, after many semesters of teaching and evaluating our own courses, we believe we have some good answers to these and many other questions that an instruction librarian, or for that matter, anyone developing an online course will have.

In *Online by Design: The Essentials of Creating Information Literacy Courses*, we share our experiences developing online information literacy courses for undergraduate and graduate students from across disciplines. Our first guiding principle throughout the book and weaved into our own course development is that pedagogy is paramount. A winning online course puts pedagogy before technology and trends. Our second guiding principle is that the pedagogy that may work wonders in the traditional classroom can fail miserably in the online environment. Developing an online course is not a simple digitization of face-to-face classroom materials, lecture, and activities. Rather it is a *transformation* of course readings, lectures, and assignments to a format that maximizes engagement and learning for students.

BOOK ORGANIZATION

We have organized *Online by Design: The Essentials of Creating Information Courses* to mimic the course development process from creating course and learning outcomes to assessing and evaluating your efforts. Thus, a sequential reading will provide you with a guide as you create your courses. However, each chapter is meant to serve as a stand-alone piece and acts as a quick reference guide to the different components of the course-development process. The first section, Developing the Course, focuses on laying out the curriculum, and the second section, Developing the Units, focuses on creating the materials and units that will allow you to meet your course goals. The two main sections of the book are further broken up into the following chapters:

Chapter 1: Introduction

In the introduction we make a case for online courses and look at both the merits and drawbacks of online information literacy courses. We also discuss the research surrounding the effectiveness of online courses and how students and faculty perceive online courses.

Section 1: Developing the Course

Chapter 2: The Nuts and Bolts of Online Credit Courses: What You Need to Know Before You Start

Developing and teaching an online course will likely take more resources and time than you will have originally anticipated. In this chapter, we look at the different roles you will play and the varied competencies you will need to have to successfully develop and teach an online course.

Chapter 3: A Recipe for Success: Cooking Up the Curriculum

Writing good course goals and student learning outcomes is the first step in creating an engaging and effective course. In this chapter we discuss how to write strong, measurable outcomes, and how to plan the curriculum with a backward approach.

Chapter 4: Creating a Student-Centered Syllabus: Taking It to the Next Level

A good syllabus not only makes students aware of important dates and exams, but it also helps to set the tone for the course and can guide students throughout it. In this chapter we look at both the roles of the traditional syllabus and how today's technologies can help you create dynamic, multimedia syllabi.

Section 2: Developing the Units

Chapter 5: Learning Materials 101: Variety Is the Spice of Life

Once you have established your learning outcomes and how you will sequence your course, it is time to start creating materials. In this chapter we look at and emphasize the need to create a variety of materials from readings and discussions to using social media tools and digital badges.

Chapter 6: Tutorials 101: Keeping Students Engaged

In this chapter we take a look at how to create engaging and interactive tutorials with an emphasis on using rapid e-learning content authoring tools. We discuss the importance of creating tutorials that include both knowledge outcomes and application of real-world skills.

Chapter 7: Assignments 101: Making It Real, Related, and Rewarding

The course assignments you create will likely count for the majority of students' efforts, and as such, they must be meaningful and authentic. In this chapter we discuss best practices in assignment development from creating scalable assignments to creating successful collaborative assignments.

Chapter 8: But Did They Learn Anything? Assessing and Evaluating

Taking the time to create good assessments, whether they are common objective-type tests or more complex performance-based activities, will become a regular part of your course-development process. In this chapter we look at different types of formative and summative assessments and give examples of best practices in each.

Chapter 9: New Models for Teaching and Learning

What will online education look like in five or ten years? In this chapter we take a look at emerging educational technologies including digital badges, Massive Open Online Courses, hybrid instruction, and offer predictions for the future of distance education.

With each passing semester, online courses become more and more popular and unlike many trends in technology, we do not see this trend subsiding. Online courses offer librarians an opportunity to teach information literacy concepts and research skills in new ways that have not traditionally been part of a library's instructional program. Additionally, the convenience and reach to so many students who could not otherwise take our courses will ensure that online courses continue to grow and improve. The many benefits of online courses only help ensure their popularity, but this popularity cannot be equated with quality or effectiveness. We hope that with this book we help librarians successfully create engaging, effective, and dynamic courses that are rooted in sound pedagogy and driven by students' needs.

Acknowledgments

This book was made possible because of the belief in the power of and need for library instruction and because of the many hours our instructional team devoted to the creation of online courses. Our course-development process has been a group effort, and we have shared the lessons learned and the successes with many current and former colleagues. We would like to thank Leslie Sult, Jeanne Pfander, Rebecca Blakiston, Keith Rocci, and Elizabeth Kline for their continued support and insights. We must also thank Laurie Eagleson for the many hours she spent making sure every aspect of our courses worked as intended. Before online courses were even a possibility, Louise Greenfield, Vicki Mills, and Ruth Dickstein made great contributions to the information literacy efforts at our institution and to the profession. Their experience and wisdom is legendary and invaluable and has guided us throughout the process.

Carla J. Stoffle first approached us with the idea of creating online credit courses and provided us with the continued support to see it through. We would also like to thank Michael Brewer for his continued leadership and advocacy for our courses. A special thank you goes to Melody Buckner, instructional designer extraordinaire and a wonderful colleague. We owe special thanks to our dean, Karen Williams, for her generosity in writing the foreword for our book. Thank you to our editor, Charles Harmon, for planting the seed for the idea of a book and working with us to see it through to its end.

Thank you to all our friends and family for their unwavering support, particularly Mary Evangeliste and Hector and Matilde Mery for their countless hours of babysitting that allowed this book to become a reality. A special thanks to Dan Lee, friend, family, and colleague, for his expertise in all matters related to copyright.

We have been lucky to have worked with an amazing group of graduate students who spent countless hours teaching courses and providing us with great feedback: thank you Ke Peng, Jennifer Holland, Bethany Maile, and Erin Armstrong. Finally, thank you to all the students who have taken our courses; they have been the best teachers.

Chapter One

Introduction

ME? TEACH AN ONLINE INFORMATION
LITERACY COURSE? BUT WHY?

In the winter of 2008, our associate dean informed us that we were moving to a new model of instruction where we would no longer offer face-to-face instruction. Like many of our colleagues, we met this declaration with disbelief, fear, a sense of dread, and many, many questions: Why teach online? Why move to a model of instruction that had not been proven to be effective? How could we give up our sacred face-to-face sessions with students? How could we move our instructional efforts online? How would students and faculty reach us? What new skills, programs, and technologies would we need to develop to be successful? These were just some of the many questions that were raised, and in this book we set out to answer these questions using our own experiences along with research studies in the area of online instruction.

In this introductory chapter, we focus on the question of why libraries should teach an online information literacy (IL) course. First, we look at online education from the perspective of students, teaching faculty, and librarians. Then, we investigate the research surrounding the effectiveness of online learning and the benefits of online credit courses. Finally, we discuss some of the challenges of teaching and learning online and provide definitions of terms we use throughout the book.

PERCEPTIONS OF ONLINE LEARNING

It was just a few years ago that online education was a new endeavor for most universities and colleges, but today online classes are commonplace across all types of higher education institutions. The percentage of students enrolled in higher education taking a least one online course went from less than 10 percent in fall 2002 to 32 percent in fall 2011.[1] The latest numbers on high school students enrolled in an online credit course was 1.3 million in 53 percent of U.S. public school districts in 2009–2010.[2] In higher education, students are showing a preference for online learning, especially in a blended environment.[3] In a national survey of undergraduate students, 40 percent of older students (age twenty-five and older) agreed that online courses were as valuable as face-to-face courses as compared to more traditional-aged under-graduates (23 percent), whereas 45 percent of all students who had taken an online course say it was as valuable as an in-classroom course.[4] Students use technology to connect with friends, their school, instructors, and courses, and as they spend more time online, they have an expectation that technology will be part of their educational experience; they also expect their instructors to use technology effectively in their classes.[5]

Even though online classes have exploded, it is often difficult to convince faculty including librarians that teaching online can be as effective as teaching in the traditional classroom. When our library moved to an online model of IL instruction many librarians resisted partially because of a belief that online instruction could not offer the same benefits of immediate feedback, demonstration, and individualized help that the classroom model could. A recent survey conducted by the Babson Survey Research Group on the perceptions of the quality of online education by teaching faculty and technology administrators found that teaching faculty are less excited and more fearful about the growth of online learning than technology administrators.[6] The teaching faculty that responded to the survey were not convinced of the effectiveness of online learning, with nearly two-thirds responding that learning outcomes in an online course were inferior or somewhat inferior to a face-to-face course. Further analysis showed that faculty who had experience teaching an online course or worked at an institution where there was a fully developed online education program were more likely to have a positive attitude toward online courses.

PERCEPTIONS OF IL CREDIT COURSES

Along with questions concerning online learning, librarians are also concerned about the efficacy of IL credit courses versus embedded instruction. In a survey of librarian perceptions of credit courses, only 30 percent of respondents indicated that they perceive such courses as being effective.[7] William Badke, and Steven Bell in his response to Badke's article on teaching credit courses, address many of the pros and cons of teaching credit IL courses.[8] Whereas Badke argues that credit courses are needed to adequately teach students crucial IL skills, Bell concludes that credit courses do not teach IL skills in the context of a student's discipline nor do they lead to IL as being seen as more credible. This debate on whether libraries should develop and teach courses is by no means a new one. In their 2012 paper, Gunselman and Blakesley review a century-old discussion on the same topic.[9] Although this debate is an old one, with the explosion of online learning it seems that it is only a matter of time for course-development efforts to be a regular part of academic libraries' instruction programs. Unfortunately, at this time there are no current numbers on how many libraries choose to offer credit courses. However, for institutions that do offer credit courses, there is trend toward offering those courses in an online format.[10]

IS ONLINE INSTRUCTION EFFECTIVE?

Although there may be anecdotal evidence and numerous factors for different perceptions of online credit IL courses, the research has shown that there is little to no difference in terms of student achievement between distance and traditional instruction. A 2004 meta-analysis of more than 230 research studies on the effectiveness of distance education versus classroom instruction found that there was no significant difference between the two types of instruction.[11] A more recent (2010) meta-analysis from the U.S. Department of Education found that students who participated in online courses performed slightly better than students who learned the same material via face-to-face instruction.[12] Similar to the previous meta-analysis, this study included distance education across disciplines and age groups. Both studies point out the difficulty of comparing online instruction to traditional forms because there are so many variables in what constitutes online learning (synchronous, asynchronous, hybrid, web facilitated, etc.).

The literature on the effectiveness of online IL courses is scarce because online library courses are not prevalent across libraries yet. In the library literature there is more of an emphasis on embedded librarianship and effectiveness of stand-alone tutorials. A 2007 systematic review of literature that compared computer-assisted instruction to face-to-face delivery by a librarian found little difference between the effectiveness of the two.[13] Of the ten studies examined, nine found no difference, and one found face-to-face instruction to be more effective. The authors also looked at affective outcomes and found mixed results toward computer-assisted instruction. For online courses, the results are similar. Burkhardt, Kinnie, and Cournoyer compared the results of an exam taken by students in a three-credit IL course.[14] The authors found that students who took the course online performed better on the test than students who took the same course in a classroom. Similarly, in our research study on learning outcomes assessment of an online course, we found that students who participated in an online course performed significantly better on a post-test than students who received a traditional one-shot librarian-led class session.[15]

The aforementioned studies and hundreds more like them show that online instruction can be as or more effective than traditional instruction. Thus, future research into online learning should focus on the types of teaching and learning activities that make it effective and not on comparing online instruction with face-to-face instruction. In this book, we set out to do just that.

BENEFITS OF ONLINE INSTRUCTION FOR STUDENTS, LIBRARIANS, AND LIBRARIES

As librarians, we know the value of students developing IL skills, and we know that few of our students enter our colleges and universities with these skills. We also know that what we call IL skills go beyond basic literacy skills; they are complex critical thinking skills of evaluation, analysis, synthesis, and reflection. Unfortunately, these skills cannot be adequately addressed in traditional one-shot sessions that rarely go beyond an hour of instruction. In contrast to the one-shot session, an IL course can provide students with both the foundational knowledge and abilities in locating information and the higher-order skills of evaluating and synthesizing information that will serve them well in their college careers and beyond. In addition to providing students with sustained IL instruction, online courses offer students more flexibility in taking courses. Many students enrolled in higher education today are nontraditional students who live off-campus, go to school part-time, have families, and work full-time. Additionally, libraries have changed considerably since nontraditional students' last college experience. Enrolling in an online IL course can give them the confidence and extra help needed to succeed in their courses. An online course also has the added benefit of a student being able to develop these skills in a safe environment at their own pace.

An obvious benefit of offering an online IL course is being able to reach more students in an anywhere, anytime environment. Because of the availability of digital resources offered by libraries, online IL courses are a natural fit for reaching students in this environment. Librarians can also create more meaningful relationships with students because they have access to the same students over an entire course, and they can use this experience to develop a deeper understanding of a student's research process. Librarians designing and teaching an online course have opportunities to learn new technologies such as the learning management system (LMS), web conferencing systems, videocasting, and different content authoring tools. Furthermore, with support from the administration, librarians can develop instructional design skills and knowledge of online pedagogy through taking courses, workshops, and attending e-learning conferences. Teaching an online credit course also offers librarians opportunities to meet and work with other teaching and learning professionals on campus.

As the trend continues for academic institutions to offer more online and hybrid courses and LMSs to evolve in their functionality and become easier to use, offering an online credit course is becoming more attractive and beneficial for a library's instructional program. As budget cuts reduce library staff, an online course is a way to offer IL instruction to more students with a smaller cadre of library staff that can include using graduate students as instructors. Another added benefit is that the online credit course can be a revenue generator for the library where there is a high enrollment of students and the library receives the student credit hour (SCH) funding.

Beyond the fiscal benefits of offering online credit courses is the increase in the reputation and standing of the library. If librarians are teaching credit courses, they are seen as teachers along with teaching faculty. An IL credit course demonstrates that IL concepts are important for students to learn and that librarians are experts in this area. It can also lead to a greater awareness of the library's ability to provide online instruction and more willingness on the part of departmental faculty to incorporate information literacy instruction into their courses.[16]

THE CHALLENGES OF ONLINE INSTRUCTION

As effective and beneficial as an online course can be, there are many issues and common pitfalls of online instruction that should be discussed.

Student Challenges

Technology Skills

Both traditional and nontraditional students often lack the technology skills needed to successfully access and navigate an online course. Even students who have taken an online course in secondary school can have difficulty navigating a new LMS. In a recent study of the use of technology by undergraduates, 66 percent of U.S. students reported that when they entered college/university they had the technology skills needed to succeed in their courses. However, in the same study, 64 percent of U.S. students stated that it was very/extremely important to develop better technology skills or get training.[17] Although students believe that they have online technology skills, an LMS is not as intuitive as many of the social network platforms they are well acquainted with. In our online courses, we have found that we often spend a great deal of time fielding questions related to the LMS. Often these types of questions surpass content questions in their frequency and amount of time it takes to answer them.

Time Management

Taking an online course takes discipline and a daily commitment to set aside time to login to the course, review the content, and complete assignments. Nontraditional students often take online courses because they need a learning experience that is flexible and does not overburden their already busy schedule. However, it can be difficult for them to find the time to access an online course even a few times a week. Similarly, younger traditional students often lack the discipline to access a course daily, much less weekly. In the online courses we have taught, we have found that many students login to the LMS as little as possible and complete assignments only a few hours or even minutes before they are due.

Lack of Motivation

Attendance, especially attendance that is graded, can be a great motivator for students. In the online class, the lack of being expected to show up to an actual classroom at a certain time can be a great disadvantage for many students. In a traditional classroom the student can ask a question in class and receive immediate feedback. In an online course, this can take hours or even days. Another demotivator that students find in online courses is the lack of community among students. In a classroom, students learn from one another during discussions and can offer each other support both inside and outside of class. Even with excellent student discussions, this sense of community is difficult to replicate online.

Technology Problems with Platforms and Networks

Another frustrating drawback is the lack of access to software programs used in online courses. We often take it for granted that students have ready access to programs such as PowerPoint, Word, or Flash. However, many students choose to use free or online programs such as OpenOffice or Google Docs. As a result, students cannot open documents and complete assignments. Often instructors have to upload several versions of the same document. In our classes, we also often encounter problems with different browsers, with Flash programs not operating correctly, and with audio issues. Network issues can also occur if the student is not able to connect to the course as a result of low-speed network connections, proxy issues, or network problems that affect the LMS or the library's servers.

Instructor Challenges

Lack of ability to get to know students in a more personalized manner is a common experience of online instructors. Without face-to-face contact, students can easily become just names on a page. For an instructor, perhaps the biggest drawback to online teaching is the absence of teachable moments. The immediacy of a face-to-face class session allows an instructor to quickly change directions if he or she notices that students are struggling with a concept. In an online class, it can take weeks or even an entire semester to understand what students are and are not grasping well. Because much of the content in an online course is developed and posted at the onset of the course, it is almost impossible to tailor a module at the last minute. Lastly, good instructors evaluate their teaching with each course they deliver. They consider what worked and did not work in the class session and where improvements can be made. For an online class, this type of reflection and evaluation cannot be addressed until the end of the semester, if at all. Other common issues that instructors have with online courses include long development time, length of time helping students with technology issues, lack of technology skills, and unfamiliarity with online pedagogy. In this book, we address detailed ways to overcome these and other common issues of online learning.

Challenges of Teaching IL Online

As with many disciplines, there are some IL skill areas that are more difficult to teach online. When we first taught our freshman-level course, we found that helping a student through the process of choosing and narrowing a topic required a two-way dialogue that was difficult to replicate online. In our current course, we have students choose from a list of topics we have already vetted. In a face-to-face course, the instructor can assess students' ability to carry out a successful search by monitoring them in real time. This same exercise in an online course requires more written instructions, and the feedback occurs long after the exercise is completed and may not even be read by the student. In this book, we offer practical advice on how to overcome these common online teaching and learning pitfalls.

DEFINING ONLINE INSTRUCTION

Before concluding this chapter, we provide definitions for different types of online instruction and the many different terms used to describe instruction that takes place in an environment other than the traditional classroom. The *Encyclopedia of Educational Psychology* defines distance learning as "the communication over distance between teacher and student mediated by print or some form of technology designed to bridge the separation between teacher and student in space or time."[18] Thus, this broad definition includes all forms of distance education from stand-alone tutorials to hybrid courses to correspondence courses. Here we offer definitions of terms that are most often used in discussions of online learning and in this book:

Online learning or *e-learning*: Distance education where learning takes place through electronic or digital means, most often over the Internet. We do not distinguish between these two terms and like many educators use them interchangeably.

Online instruction: In contrast to online learning that focuses on what the student does, online instruction refers to the activities of the instructor from development of materials to delivery to assessment.

Hybrid or *blended courses*: Courses that include both online and face-to-face elements. In this category, we do not include typical college courses that have regularly scheduled classroom instruction but that use an LMS for productivity activities, such as tracking grades and posting readings. We do include courses that are offered predominantly online but may have some element of required face-to-face time such as class meetings or group work.

Synchronous: Online instruction that takes place in real time. Holding a web conference using a tool, such as Adobe Connect or holding a class session in a chat room, are examples of synchronous activities.

Asynchronous: Online instruction that takes place at different times. Watching a PowerPoint lecture or writing a response to a discussion board in an LMS are examples of asynchronous activities. An advantage of asynchronous activities is that they can occur at any time.

E-learning 2.0: In contrast to e-learning, which is created and led by an instructor, e-learning 2.0 can be constructed and led by students and makes use of Web 2.0 technologies such as blogs and wikis. In their paper on e-learning, Huang and Shiu describe it as "a kind of collaborative and user-centric learning, which is based on collective intelligence rather than a few experts' knowledge."[19]

Learning Objects: Similar to learning materials, a learning object is a broad term for items such as guides, tutorials, assignments, and quizzes that one could use for learning and teaching online.

Learning Management Systems (LMSs): An LMS is an online tool that allows instructors to post and deliver content to students. Most LMSs are robust tools that in addition to posting of content also allows for grade tracking, test taking, and communicating with students in different formats. Although there are some differences between LMSs and course management systems, we use the terms synonymously. Popular LMSs include Moodle, Blackboard Learn, Desire2Learn, and eCollege.

KNOW THIS . . .

- Online education is here to stay and will continue to grow in higher education.
- Research shows that online learning can be as effective as face-to-face learning.
- IL skills include complex, higher-order thinking skills that take time to learn and develop.
- An IL online course gives students the time and type of environment needed to develop these complex skills.
- There are many challenges to online education, but with planning, many can be successfully overcome.
- Online credit courses allow libraries to reach more students with the same or possibly less resources.
- An online IL credit course can increase the stature of a library on campus.

NOTES

1. I. Elaine Allen and Jeff Seaman, *Changing Course: Ten Years of Tracking Online Education in the United States* (Babson Survey Research Group and Quahog Research Group LLC, 2013), http://www.onlinelearningsurvey.com/.

2. Susan Aud, et al., *The Condition of Education 2012 (NCES 2012-045)* (Washington, DC: U.S. Department of Education, National Center for Education, 2012), http://nces.ed.gov/pubsearch.

3. Eden Dahlstrom, et al., *The ECAR National Study of Undergraduate Students and Information Technology,* Research Report, (Boulder, CO: EDUCAUSE Center for Applied Research, 2011), http://www.educause.edu/ecar.

4. Eden Dahlstrom, *ECAR Study of Undergraduate Students and Information Technology, 2012.* (Louisville: EDUCAUSE Center for Applied Research, 2012).

5. Dahlstrom, et al., "The ECAR National Study."

6. I. Elaine Allen, et al., *Conflicted: Faculty and Online Education, 2012.* (The Babson Survey Research Group and Inside Higher Ed, 2012), available at http://www.insidehighered.com/sites/default/server_files/survey/conflicted.html, accessed on January 15, 2014.

7. Erin L. Davis, Kacy Lundstrom, and Pamela N. Martin, "Librarian Perceptions and Information Literacy Instruction Models," *Reference Services Review* 39, no. 4 (2011): 686–702.

8. William Badke. "Ten Reasons to Teach Information Literacy for Credit," *Online* 32, no. 6 (Nov/Dec 2008): 47–49; Steven Bell, "IL Course Credit Does Not Equal Credibility," *ACRLog,* (November 25, 2008), available at http://acrlog.org/2008/11/25/il-course-credit-does-not-equal-credibility/, accessed January 15, 2014.

9. Cheryl Gunselman and Elizabeth Blakesley, "Enduring Visions of Instruction in Academic Libraries: A Review of a Spirited Early Twentieth-Century Discussion," *portal: Libraries and the Academy* 12, no. 3 (July 2012): 259–281.

10. Margaret Burke, "Academic Libraries and the Credit-Bearing Class," *Communications in Information Literacy* 5, no. 2 (2012): 156–173.

11. Robert M. Bernard, et al., "How Does Education Compare with Classroom Instruction? A Meta-Analysis of the Empirical Literature," *Review of Educational Research* 74, no. 3 (2004): 379–439.

12. Barbara Means, et al., *Evaluation of Evidence-Based Practices in Online Learning: A Meta-Analysis and Review of Online Learning Studies,* (Washington DC: U.S. Department of Education, 2010), www.ed.gov/about/offices/list/opepd/ppss/reports.html.

13. Li Zhang, Erin M. Watson, and Laura Banfield, "The Efficacy of Computer-Assisted Instruction Versus Face-to-Face Instruction in Academic Libraries: A Systematic Review," *The Journal of Academic Librarianship* 33, no. 4 (2007): 478–484.

14. Joanna M. Burkhardt, Jim Kinnie, and Carina Cournoyer, "Information Literacy Successes Compared: Online vs. Face to Face," *Journal of Library Administration* 48, no. 3/4 (2008): 379–389.

15. Yvonne Mery, Jill Newby, and Ke Peng, "Why One-shot Information Literacy Sessions Are Not the Future of Instruction: A Case for Online Credit Courses," *College & Research Libraries* 73, no. 4 (2012): 366–377.

16. Jeanne R. Davidson, "Faculty and Student Attitudes toward Credit Courses for Library Skills," *College & Research Libraries* 62, no. 2 (2001): 155–163; Davis, et al., "Librarian Perceptions."

17. Dahlstrom, et al., "ECAR Study of Undergraduate Students."

18. Michael H. McVey, "Distance Learning," In *Encyclopedia of Educational Psychology*, edited by Neil J. Salkind, (Thousand Oaks: SAGE Publications, Inc., 2008), 262–268.

19. Huang Shiu-Li and Shiu Jung-Hung, "A User-Centric Adaptive Learning System for E-Learning 2.0," *Journal of Educational Technology & Society* 15, no. 3 (2012): 214–225, available at http://www.ifets.info/journals/15_3/16.pdf, accessed January 15, 2014.

Section One

DEVELOPING THE COURSE

Chapter Two

The Nuts and Bolts of Online Credit Courses: What You Need to Know before You Start

When we developed our first online IL course, we were energized and hopeful but also quite naive about the time, resources, and competencies we would need to create a high-quality course. There was a general belief among librarians and administrators that we would just be transferring our face-to-face sessions to an online format. Some believed that after initial development the course would take care of itself because it was all online. Furthermore, many of us mistakenly thought that an online course would free up time the librarians had previously spent developing and delivering face-to-face sessions. We have since come to learn that nothing could be further from the truth. In retrospect, it would have been useful to do some exploration and planning to give us a better sense of the time, resources, and skills we would need before taking on this endeavor.

An ideal course-development plan would include a diverse group of team members with varied skills and expertise. However, a team approach to course development is rare in many academic departments and even rarer in libraries. Unlike development of courses in other academic units where there is often more support and resources for online course development, the library and the librarian are unique in that they may very well be completely on their own to both develop and deliver a course. In this chapter, we describe the process for getting the course approved and discuss the varied roles, competencies, and time commitments a library will encounter when developing a course for the first time. We also provide an overview of the LMS functionality and take a look at where to get help designing quality courses.

THE COURSE APPROVAL PROCESS

Once your library has made the decision to offer an online course, you will need to prepare a strategy for gaining support that is based on an environmental scan of the current curriculum and input from faculty and students that identifies the existing needs and opportunities. Changes in campus leadership, new directions for general education, and a push for more online course offerings are all opportunities for making a case for an information literacy credit course. You will also need support from your library dean or director and others in top administrative library positions who can present the rationale to campus administration groups that oversee curricular policies and approval for new courses. This may take numerous contacts and approaches over a number of years.

Getting a new course approved and in the course catalog involves considerable time and planning. The process for getting a course approved and "on the books" will differ from institution to institution but will most likely follow a procedure as the one described here. If your library is just beginning to offer credit courses, you will need to first establish the library as a course-bearing entity. Often this begins with establishing a library (departmental) curriculum committee. At our institution, the curriculum committee was set up as part of our library faculty shared governance organization. The curriculum committee developed a procedure for new and revised course approvals, created a checklist for submission requirements, and provided additional pedagogical resources and a sample syllabus. Once the new/revised course request is approved by the library curriculum committee, it is forwarded to the appropriate undergraduate, graduate, or general education curriculum committee for approval.

If you are fortunate to work at a library that already has credit-bearing status, many of the procedures and course administrative duties will be familiar. If not, you may need to train yourself or an administrative assistant in the electronic course approval submission system. In any case, review the requirements for course approval for new or changed courses early on so that you can plan your timeline for course development and course approval. Take note of deadlines for course additions, changes, and deletions. Library staff involved in initiating the new course request will need to have the library department head, or the library dean, provide department/ college level administrative approval. Once the course is approved, you must go through the process of getting it added to the course catalog and the class schedule. There may also be a separate procedure for requesting an LMS course site.

ONLINE INSTRUCTOR ROLES

In a traditional face-to-face library session, a librarian plays two major roles that are also present in the online course: instructor and content expert or subject specialist. These roles also occur in the online course, but there are many other roles the librarian will have to undertake. The list presented here is not exhaustive but does cover a wide range of roles the librarian should expect to fill to some extent.

Instructional Designer

The instructional designer (ID) is the key to transforming content into a sequence of pedagogically sound, effective, and engaging activities for the student. Online learning is not equivalent to teaching with technology nor is it a mere transfer of content from one medium to another. Rather it is a transformation of content into a different learning experience. The similarities between a one-shot face-to-face IL session and a course module have little in common except for the content. The student activities, instructor demonstrations and lectures, checks for comprehension, and assessment will look different in an effective online course. In the role of ID, the librarian will develop course goals and student learning outcomes, sequence those outcomes along with other student activities, select readings, create tutorials and assessments, and plan a mechanism for evaluating the course and making changes as needed.

Subject Matter Expert

Often referred to as a subject matter expert (SME) in the literature, the SME is the content expert. In libraries, a SME is the subject librarian with a specialization in specific disciplinary areas. The SME often works closely with the ID to develop lessons and materials. The SME/ID development team is an excellent approach to course development and can produce the most effective courses because it is made up of a pedagogical and a content expert. When we needed to develop a course module for our history department, we worked closely with a history librarian and history faculty to create course goals, and the history librarian provided us with a great amount of content and knowledge aimed at where students would most likely experience problems. We then turned the goals and content into an engaging tutorial that presented students with different scenarios to work through. This work was one of the most satisfying online teaching experiences we have had and it produced excellent results. However, we have only worked in this manner a handful of times, and most likely in developing the online course you will have to play both roles.

Technology Specialist

Developing and teaching an online IL course requires a librarian or a team of librarians with varied technology skills. You will most likely learn and use more technologies than you ever anticipated. However, before you begin, you should have a firm grasp on the following core technology tools and systems:

- Microsoft Office: You will need to know how to use Word and PowerPoint to not only create materials, but you should also be prepared to answer student questions about them.
- Alternative Office applications: Many students will choose not to use Office applications and will alternatively use open source applications such as OpenOffice, Google Docs, and Prezi. Although you may not need to be proficient in these other applications, you should be aware of some of the alternatives and recognize different file formats.
- Communication tools: Many educators are turning to tools that are more robust and easier to use than many of the more popular LMSs adopted by higher education institutions. Often LMSs are quite limited in how they allow students and instructors to communicate. You should be familiar with social networking sites including blogging and wiki sites, web conferencing applications, and other education related social networking sites.
- Multimedia applications: Although you do not need to know how to use Flash or JavaScript, you should have a working knowledge of at least one tool where you can create multimedia interactive tools. Thanks to new rapid e-learning tools, such as Adobe Captivate, Lectora, and Articulate, creating tutorials with animations, interactivity, and quizzes is much easier.
- Image and video tools: You should have a basic working knowledge of video and photo software to create and edit images. Many times when we find a chart or image we want to use, we find that we need to change something minor on it to use it for our specific purposes. Having access to a database of images can aid in this area. You should also know how to upload, download, or link to videos on YouTube or another video-sharing site.
- Web development tools: Having a basic understanding of HTML or experience working with an HTML editor will save you time and will allow you to customize your course materials. LMSs do a great job of containing and delivering your content, but they are not known for their content creation functionality.
- LMS: Once all materials including readings, lectures, quizzes, and tutorials have been created, they need to be uploaded into the LMS and linked to the appropriate folders. This work includes setting up the grade book, linking assignments to the grade book, controlling the settings for availability of module content, assignments, and quizzes and when they close, and routine

quality control to ensure that all links are working. In our library, we have one librarian with an excellent attention to detail responsible for ensuring that everything gets uploaded into the LMS and works correctly.

Course Administrator

As course administrator, you will be charged with making sure the course appears in the course catalog and the schedule of classes each semester. As such you will need to have a thorough understanding of the registration and course scheduling policies and procedures. Additionally, you will need to be familiar with ordering and processing teacher course evaluations. Because many libraries do not have the staff to fill traditional course administrative roles similar to other academic departments, it is often the case that you as the instructor will need to be knowledgeable and competent in carrying out these tasks.

Student Technology Support

A large amount of the time that we dedicate to teaching our online courses is devoted to answering student questions about how to navigate the course site despite our best efforts to make the course as transparent and user friendly as possible. Your IL online course may well be the first online course your students take, and as such, students will undoubtedly get confused about how to access materials, where to place assignments, and how to post discussions. Even if students have experience with online courses, they may still experience confusion because of an unfamiliar LMS or a different course layout. Although much of this confusion can be cleared up with good navigation and directions, you should be ready to answer questions concerning browser settings, formatting documents, and in general, getting things to work as they should.

Advisor

Another unexpected role we have undertaken is that of the college advisor. Many freshman students enrolled in our courses are not yet familiar with the registration process and policies regarding grades, adding and dropping courses, and major requirements. Much time in the beginning of the semester is spent meeting with students who need to add or drop the course or have questions about their schedule. We have also fielded questions regarding major requirements, replacing grades, and financial aid issues. Again, either getting to know the policies ahead of time or knowing where to send students is critical to managing the course. Another part of the advisor role is that of the advisor/counselor. Although not such an issue in our graduate course, in our undergraduate course, we have had students come to us to discuss family, relationships, and medical problems that are getting in the way of their courses. Communication and a sympathetic ear are important here. We have also had to report students who exhibited erratic and somewhat violent behavior to the Dean of Students. Additionally, you should also be familiar with the Family Educational Rights and Privacy Act (FERPA) of 197) regulations, disability resources, and the code of student conduct.

Department Liaison

If you are developing a course for a specific subject area, you will need to work closely with that department's faculty to develop the course and the materials. When we designed disciplinary course modules, we worked with several faculty from the history department to develop course goals and create appropriate learning materials. We were also given instructor status in their course sites to create a pre- and post-test to measure student learning. Although this approach to course development helps to create a course that is better aligned with specific subject assignments, it can be much more time consuming than developing a general IL course.

Assessment Specialist

To create both formative and summative assessment tools that measure student progress, you will need to have a basic knowledge of test development. Many librarians have little experience developing assessment tools because they are accustomed to delivering one-shot sessions that are not often assessed at the student learning outcome level. We stress the importance of developing high-quality quizzes and tests that are quicker to grade than more authentic measures, such as annotated bibliographies that librarians may be more familiar with. Additionally, if you would like to know more about how students are doing in particular areas and possibly diagnose student problem areas, you will need to conduct a statistical analysis of the assessment data. Furthermore, if you are interested in developing a research study that measures student progress, you will also want to develop a knowledge of statistical analyses that goes beyond descriptive statistics.

Marketer

Often neither students nor advisors are aware that our library offers courses. If your course is not mandatory for any majors, you will need to publicize it widely. To maximize our enrollment we have taken on the roles of graphic designer to create recruitment materials and marketer to make the campus community aware of our course offerings. We have also worked with our marketing department to create high-quality print and digital materials.

Project Manager

Because development and delivery of a course can be a lengthy process that includes many tasks and may include the participation of staff from across the library, experience in project management can prove invaluable. Many times the librarian who will ultimately teach the course will also lead the course development process. The project manager will need to form a work team, set goals and deadlines, assign tasks, and ensure the project meets the timeframe and outcomes established in the beginning of the project planning process.

Instructor

As the instructor you will play all the roles listed here, but we have not yet addressed traditional instructor activities that will take up most of your time. These activities include monitoring discussions, assigning grades, answering content-related questions, reminding students of upcoming due dates, and making any necessary changes to the course content. It should be noted that although these duties are the main duties of the instructor, the aforementioned roles are important and will be part of any instructor's daily teaching duties.

Graduate Assistant Supervisor

Early on in our online course development, we decided to hire graduate assistants to teach our undergraduate course because of the large number of students and sections. As IL librarians, we develop and revise the course and all of the materials, but we have graduate students teach the course on a daily basis. Each semester that we offer the course, we also offer training sessions to new graduate teaching assistants and meet with them each week to go over any issues in the course. Sensitive issues such as student complaints about grades and course content are fielded to the supervising librarian. The use of a graduate assistant to teach the course has allowed us to free up much time during the week while still feeling confident that we are delivering a quality course.

COMPETENCIES

Pedagogy

Many faculty, including librarians with little experience in how to design effective online courses, must often take on the responsibility of developing these courses. A 2013 survey of libraries found that the majority of employers see instruction as an important part of the library.[1] However, many librarians do not have formal training in instruction, much less in instructional design. As one survey responder noted, "new librarians are thrown into the profession with very little instructional training."[2] Without proper training the instruction librarian is merely a presenter of information and not a facilitator of learning.

Good online pedagogy is rooted in good instruction and is independent of the medium used to deliver it. Effective online instruction, like effective traditional instruction, starts with a clear understanding of the students and their needs and the ability to develop learning goals to meet those needs. The instructor must also know how to develop engaging activities where students of different abilities and learning preferences can learn from one another, from their instructor, and through practice and application of newly acquired skills and knowledge. The instructor must also know how to assess student learning throughout the course and provide the student with consistent feedback on their progress. The instructor must ensure that students feel comfortable to express themselves and take risks in the classroom or online learning environment. Finally, an effective instructor should be familiar with adult learning theories that emphasize presenting students with material that builds on prior experience and knowledge and that is relevant to their lives. Adult learners, whether undergraduates or graduates, want to learn skills that are immediately applicable to their studies and lives.

A good starting point to understanding what works in college courses should begin with a reading and understanding of Chickering and Gamson's principles for effective undergraduate education.[3] Although these well-known and often cited principles are not specifically aimed at online courses, they offer a foundation for best practices across all instructional settings. Chickering and Gamson's seven principles for best practices in undergraduate teaching and learning are:

1. Encourages Contact between Students and Faculty: In our undergraduate course, students have commented how in touch they are with the instructor, our graduate teaching assistant. The teaching assistant has done an excellent job of understanding who these students are and the type of help they need both in and outside of the class. For example, the teaching assistant has helped students with financial aid questions, registration questions, and questions about which major they should pursue.

2. Encourages Cooperation among Students: The online classroom does not immediately lend itself to networking between students. However, a good instructor can encourage student cooperation through the use of group

work where students work together in teams throughout the semester to complete a project that involves problem solving.

3. Encourages Active Learning: Chickering and Gamson discuss active learning in terms of processing and applying new knowledge and skills. This is in contrast to passive learning that asks little from the learner except for the intake of information. In the online IL course, active learning can be achieved through the development of tutorials and assignments that ask students to apply IL skills in different environments, such as searching a variety of databases.

4. Gives Prompt Feedback: Instructor feedback allows students to know if they are on the right track and what they need to focus on. The need for timely feedback is even more important in online courses because students do not have the opportunity to ask clarifying questions during a lecture or meeting with an instructor after the class session. Students need to feel that the instructor is aware of them and their progress throughout the course via specific feedback in the form of discussion posts or evaluation of assignments.

5. Emphasizes Time on Task: Similar to instructors with heavy workloads, students also have limited time to devote to the course. It is easy for students to procrastinate, and the result is rushed and sloppy work. A good instructor must encourage students to regularly visit the course site through extrinsic and intrinsic motivation and not waste students' time when they do log in. Thus, a good instructor develops activities and assignments that maximize student learning time.

6. Communicates High Expectations: If you expect less from your students, they will deliver less. Often students are crunched for time and will only do the bare minimum to pass the course. However, if you expect more from your students, they will deliver more. Your expectations should be presented in the syllabus and elsewhere with clear explanations for how to meet those expectations and consequences for not meeting them. Setting clear expectations for students will allow them to better understand where they need to place their time and effort.

7. Respects Diverse Talents and Ways of Learning: Each semester that we teach our IL courses we are amazed at how different the students are from one another. Online courses, especially undergraduate courses, include students from diverse backgrounds with diverse educational experiences and diverse preparedness. A good instructor is able to engage all students through a variety of activities and assignments that are created for diverse backgrounds and learning preferences.

Communication

In addition to knowledge of best teaching practices, the online instructor must also be an excellent communicator, especially in written form. Good communication is woven throughout the online instructor's tasks from developing learning goals that are written clearly and can be understood by students to daily informal e-mail communication and news postings. Students often tend to scan digital text; as a result, there is a need for clarity and brevity in all communication with students. The instructor must have excellent interpersonal communication skills because they may also be required to respond to a wide variety of student personal issues that call for understanding and sensitivity.

Organization and Time Management

The LMS allows for much easier organization of online course content and materials than what is typically encountered in a face-to-face course. With an online course, there is no need to keep a paper grade book to track students, no need to collect student papers in class and take them back to the office for grading, and no need to distribute paper handouts. However, use of an LMS still requires strong organizational skills and an attention to detail. You will need to organize course materials and student work in readily available digital files, and you will need to store files both locally and in the LMS. It is also wise to keep an archive file of all student communication. Time management is also necessary to ensure that assignments are graded and feedback is provided in a timely fashion and that you are able to respond quickly to student questions both through the LMS course site and by e-mail messaging.

The aforementioned competencies are in no way an exhaustive list of competencies for the online librarian, but they are some of the most crucial competencies for successful online teaching. The Pennsylvania State University has developed a Faculty Self-Assessment for Online Teaching survey[4] that addresses many competencies across broader skill areas including organization, time management, and teaching. The survey provides excellent and detailed feedback on how prepared you are and which competencies you may need to work on.

TIME COMMITMENT

One question we are consistently asked by others is "how long does it take?" Unfortunately, this is not an easy question to answer because how long an online course or course module will take to develop and teach depends on a multitude of factors, including how many people are involved in the development of the course and the skills and experience each of them brings. What we can say for certain, is that it will take longer than you expect and longer to develop and deliver than a traditional face-to-face course. Key findings from a 2004 survey of online instructors emphasize this point.[5] In this survey, faculty reported that they spent an average of 18.25 hours a week teaching an online course. Much of this time is devoted to student communication. This same survey points out that students in online courses expect their instructors to be more readily available to answer student questions compared to students in face-to-face courses. In our courses, we have included a communication statement that students can expect a response within twenty-four hours. This quick turnaround time is needed because students are often not able to complete an assignment until they get their question answered. In terms of course development, it has been our experience that you should plan for development at least six months in advance. When our university began an online course development initiative, instructors new to online course development found that they needed a semester plus a summer to fully develop a course.

MARKETING THE COURSE

Students, faculty, and advisors will most likely be unaware that your library offers courses; much less that it offers a new online course. As such, to attract students, you will need to advertise the course broadly to your campus. Our graphic artist helped us to create digital and print material that we could use throughout campus (see Figures 2.1 and 2.2). Some of the strategies we have used to market our online course are:

- Meet with administrators to inquire about how to reach students and make them aware of the course so the information can trickle down to faculty and advisors.
- Advertise the course during workshops, orientations, and instructional sessions.
- Send an e-mail message to faculty you know who would be interested in directing their students to the course.
- Send a message through a mailing list to academic advisors during key registration periods.
- Target students already enrolled in online programs.
- Advertise the course on social networking sites such as Twitter and Facebook.

Figure 2.1. Marketing Materials for an Undergraduate Course
Reprinted courtesy of The Arizona Board of Regents for the University of Arizona. Art direction: Marty Taylor; design: John Stobbe; chalkboard image: Jay Lopez; copyright HAAP Media Ltd., used by permission.

Figure 2.2. Marketing Materials for a Graduate Course
Source: Reprinted courtesy of The Arizona Board of Regents for the University of Arizona. Design: Marty Taylor.

- Advertise the course on the library's homepage.
- Place flyers in library study areas including study carrels and any areas with high student traffic.
- Create a digital slide announcing your new course for your library's digital announcement system.
- Develop a web page where you can provide more information about the syllabus.

THE LMS: A LOVE/HATE RELATIONSHIP

The LMS will be the software tool you will most often work with, and it will most likely lead to both appreciation and endless frustration. LMSs are robust systems that are often lacking in their intuitiveness. We have used several LMSs to develop courses and there is always a learning curve with each one. Whether you must use your institution's licensed LMS or have the freedom to choose an open source system, you should spend time becoming familiar with it as both a student and an instructor. You should also identify who to contact to get help with troubleshooting problems. Your LMS is not just a tool to distribute content to students; it has a multitude of functionalities that will save you time and help organize your content in meaningful ways. Your LMS should allow for automatic grading of items, creating different types of quizzes, easily copying materials from one section to another and from one semester to another, and tracking the time students spend in your course. This tracking feature should also include the ability to see what content students access and the length of time they spend with that content. An LMS should also allow for communication between students and between students and the instructor in a number of ways in addition to e-mail and discussion posts. As mentioned previously many LMSs fall short in this area and do not offer more robust ways of communication such as blogs, wikis, and video conferencing. Other recommended functionalities are:

- Sharable Content Object Reference Model (SCORM) compliant
- Universal design features that make content and communication accessible to all students
- Lockers for students to store their own work
- RSS feeds
- Podcast creation and distribution
- Mobile accessibility options
- Ability to support interactive Flash programs
- Integration of popular social networking sites such as Twitter or Facebook
- Customization of different labels or tabs
- A single sign on system for authentication and authorization

Another frustration with LMSs is their lack of a clear navigational interface for both students and instructors. We begin our undergraduate course with a focus on the LMS and getting to know it through exercises and videos. However, we still encounter a multitude of questions from students on how to use specific tools and complete certain tasks. Even though you may set up your course to be as clear and organized as possible, with technology you cannot anticipate every possible problem a student may encounter. Setting up the grade book in an LMS can also be a daunting task because of the many different options and unclear vocabulary the LMS may employ. We have seen many instructors choose to enter their grades into the grade book manually instead of setting up automatic grading at the onset of the course. The ability to easily create different types of quizzes should be a key function of the LMS. However, we have experienced many problems with editing questions and reusing them in other LMS course sites, and importing and exporting questions is a convoluted and time-consuming process. In other words, you will experience technology issues with whatever LMS you are using.

QUALITY MATTERS!

As you prepare to create your online course and move it into the LMS, it is useful to think about an overall design plan for your course. For our online courses, we used the research-based pedagogical principles from the Quality Matters (QM) program.[6] The QM program is a national organization that provides faculty peer-review certification of quality online and blended courses. The foundation of the QM program is a set of standards and rubrics based on meta-analysis of research studies into best practices in online education. The QM standards and rubrics are used to evaluate the organization and navigation of the course, learning objectives, learning materials, student engagement, assessment and evaluation, technology, student support, and accessibility. An important element of the QM standards is alignment between learning objectives, learning materials and activities, technology, and assessment.

We were introduced to the QM through working collaborations with an instructional design specialist who serves as the institutional representative for the QM program. We attended campus workshops and completed the QM Peer Review certification program to become external QM peer reviewers. These online training courses provided a relatively inexpensive and quick way to learn about best practices in online course design. In addition, we have been invited to conduct informal reviews of newly developed online courses offered through a grant-funded online course development program at our institution. We have applied the QM rubrics in the design of our IL online courses and have included elements of QM rubrics throughout this book. To determine if your institution is a subscriber to the QM program, the QM Program web site provides a list of institution and state-wide consortia subscribers.

WHERE TO GET TRAINING

One of the best ways to become familiar with online course design is to take an online course. You will quickly learn what works and what does not in an online learning environment. There are many opportunities to enroll in an online course through your institution, the American Library Association, the Association of College and Research Libraries, or through a massive open online course (MOOC). These courses need not be directly related to information literacy or librarianship because taking an online course in another subject that interests you will allow you to more fully experience the course from a student's perspective. Taking an online course will also allow you to see how other instructors organize their courses and the different strategies they employ. Other useful organizations that offer training and workshops in online instruction include Educause and the eLearning Guild.

KNOW THIS . . .

- The development of an online course will take more time and resources than you will initially anticipate. You should plan on spending at least six months developing your course.
- New courses will need to go through a lengthy campus course approval process.
- As an online instructor you will take on many roles that are not found in a traditional librarian position.
- Hiring and training a graduate assistant to help teach the course will save time.
- Effective and successful online teaching requires competencies in the areas of pedagogy, communication, and management.
- Students of online courses expect their instructors to be more readily available than students in face-to-face courses.
- Most LMSs will not meet all of your instructional needs, and you may need to use other tools to create content and communicate with students.
- To make students, faculty, and advisors aware of your course, you will need to develop a marketing plan.

• Quality Matters is a nationally recognized program that provides opportunities for online course evaluation and professional development in effective course design.

NOTES

1. Russell A. Hall, "Beyond the Job Ad: Employers and Library Instruction," *College & Research Libraries* 74, no. 1 (2013): 24–38.
2. Ibid.
3. Arthur W. Chickering, and Zelda F. Gamson, *Applying the Seven Principles for Good Practice in Undergraduate Education* (San Francisco: Jossey-Bass, 1991).
4. "Faculty Self-Assessment for Online Teaching," Pennsylvania State University, https://weblearning.psu.edu/FacultySelfAssessment/.
5. Morris T. Keeton, "Best Online Instructional Practices: Report of Phase I of an Ongoing Study," *Journal of Asynchronous Learning Networks* 8, no. 2 (Apr 2004): 75–100.
6. "Quality Matters," Quality Matters Program, http://www.qmprogram.org/.

SUGGESTED READINGS

Bigatel, Paula Mae, Lawrence C. Ragan, Shannon Kennan, Janet May, and Brian F. Redmond. "The Identification of Competencies for Online Teaching Success." *Journal of Asynchronous Learning Networks* 16, no. 1 (January 2012): 59–77.
Henry, Jim, and Jeff Meadows. "An Absolutely Riveting Online Course: Nine Principles for Excellence in Web-Based Teaching." *Canadian Journal of Learning and Technology* 34, no. 1 (2008), available at http://www.cjlt.ca/index.php/cjlt/article/view/179/177, accessed January 15, 2014.
Hollister, Christopher Vance, ed. *Best Practices for Credit-bearing Information Literacy Courses.* Chicago: Association of College and Research Libraries, 2010.
Keeton, Morris T., Barry G. Sheckley, and Joan Kejci Griggs. *Effectiveness and Efficiency in Higher Education for Adults: A Guide for Fostering Learning.* Dubuque, IA: Kendall/Hunt Publishing Company, 2002.
Pallof, Rena M., and Keith Pratt. *Lessons from the Cyberspace Classroom: The Realities of Online Teaching.* San Francisco: Jossey-Bass, 2001.
Smith, Theodore C. "Fifty-One Competencies for Online Instruction." *The Journal of Educators Online* 2, no. 2 (July 2005), available at http://www.thejeo.com/Ted%20Smith%20Final.pdf, accessed January 15, 2014.

Chapter Three

A Recipe for Success:
Cooking Up the Curriculum

Have you ever taken a really good course? One that changed the way you think or one where you mastered a new skill. One that got you so excited that you wanted to find out as much additional information about the subject as you could? Much of what made that course great was the deliberate selection of content by the instructor. We titled this chapter "A Recipe for Success" because like a good dish that is dependent on a careful selection of ingredients and how those ingredients are combined, curriculum development is dependent on the topics you include, what you leave out, and how you put everything together. This will in turn help determine how dynamic and effective your course is. However, deciding what topics to include and how to present them to students can be a difficult task.

In this chapter we get down to the design of the course curriculum: selecting the ingredients that will go into your course and how you will mix them all together. When creating a curriculum, there are a number of components that must be addressed and must work together for a consistent and cohesive curriculum. These include:

- student needs
- course goals
- student learning outcomes
- unit sequencing
- learning materials
- learning activities
- learning outcomes assessments
- course evaluation

In this chapter, we discuss gathering information about your students' knowledge and abilities, how to develop course goals and learning outcomes based on the Association of College and Research Libraries (ACRL) standards, selecting course topics, and scoping and sequencing units. We will also take a look at considerations for using a textbook and provide samples of our own information literacy course curricula.

NEEDS ASSESSMENT AND ENVIRONMENTAL SCANNING

What Do Your Students Know?

One of the most popular approaches to instructional design is the AD-DIE model that prescribes a circular process of design. ADDIE stands for Analysis, Design, Development, Implementation, and Evaluation. In an ideal situation, the first step in the ADDIE model, analysis, would begin with a thorough needs assessment where you could gather information on students' needs and skill levels. However, in designing an IL course you will not have access to your potential students to test their knowledge and abilities. Additionally, most IL students come from disciplines across campus with varying degrees of expertise and experiences. Although testing students before your course may be impossible, you probably already know a lot about them from working the reference desk, delivering instructional sessions and workshops, and talking with faculty. Asking yourself the following questions can help in getting to know your students:

- Are they undergraduates or graduate students?
- What year in school are most of them in?
- Are they from a specific discipline?
- What is their level of technical skills?
- What technologies are they already familiar with?
- What kinds of technology do they use regularly?
- What kinds of technology do they have access to?
- From your reference desk activities, what do you see students struggling with?
- How do they like to learn?
- What are their prior experiences with research?
- Have they taken online courses?
- How do they feel about online courses?

Environmental scanning at the local and national level can also help you answer questions about the need for the course and how it aligns with your institution's goals. These questions include:

- What is the context for offering this course?
- Why is it needed?
- What are the emerging education trends on college campuses and possible shifts in institutional focus and strategies for student success and retention that your course could fulfill?
- Are there new campus programs that you could align with your new online IL course?

The results of your needs assessment and environmental scan will determine unmet needs that will make your course more viable.

When we began planning our online graduate course, our first task was to determine if IL-related concepts were being taught in disciplinary research methods courses on campus. We reviewed research methods course descriptions and talked with faculty who taught graduate students. We discovered that there were no research methods courses that covered IL topics. We knew that we could fill a big gap in what graduate students needed to know about information research strategies and management and use of information for writing their theses or dissertation. We also knew that the course curriculum would need to go beyond the basic IL concepts presented at graduate student orientations and one-shot classroom sessions.

WRITING GOALS AND OUTCOMES

Backward Curriculum Design

Traditional curriculum design often starts with the content. For example, in traditional curriculum design, a history professor teaching a course in European history would lay out the curriculum by looking at major time periods and topics and then sequencing them in chronological order. In contrast, the method that we recommend follows a backward approach to curriculum design that begins with a look at the end result. That is, at what you want your students to look like at the end of your course. The needs assessment provides you with a good idea of students' behavior at the beginning of the course, but you also need a good idea of students' behavior after taking your course. We recommend starting the curriculum development process by thinking about what you would like to observe in your students after taking your course. To get started, ask yourself questions such as:

- What behaviors would I like to see in my students after they complete my course?

- What concepts and theories will students know after taking the course?
- What terminology will students understand and use?
- How will they feel about research at the end of my course?

Another method that can help you gain a better understanding of what you want your end results to look like is to create a persona of a student that describes them after taking your course. As you begin to describe the student you can ask yourself the preceding questions. Here we have included before and after personas for a student in our undergraduate course.

Before Course Persona

Emma is a freshman student who is new to the city. She is not sure of her major but is thinking of pursuing a degree related to nutrition and food science. Emma is not familiar with the library or its resources. In the past when she had to write research papers, she started with Google, which usually lead to a Wikipedia entry. If she could not find what she needed using Google (rarely), she occasionally visited her school library for a book. Emma likes the convenience of using web resources and does not see a need to use material that is not available through Google. She finds research tedious and is often overwhelmed by what she finds which is why she likes to select the first few links she encounters. She usually begins a research project by writing and then filling in the pieces with sources if her professor requires them.

After Course Persona

Emma starts her research by free writing on the topic and getting some thoughts out on paper. She realizes that she does not know a lot about the topic and must first get some background information. She begins her research at the library web site, accesses a subject guide, and then looks for an encyclopedia article. After reading the encyclopedia article and taking some notes, she moves on to using different databases. She is actively searching and changes her search strategies as she looks through her results. She occasionally asks a librarian for help via chat. Emma does not like having to go to the library to pick up a book so she sticks with digital formats that she knows how to download or request. Emma reads the sources she finds and takes notes, jotting down new things she learns, what she agrees and does not agree with, and how she may use the source in her paper. Emma's research paper indicates that she cites her sources accurately and uses a variety of sources. The text of her paper and her uses of sources in it also indicates that she has synthesized what she has read and has used her sources purposefully.

Once you have a thorough understanding of your students and their needs, you can move on to creating course goals. Goals are broad statements that describe the overall purpose of the course. They are generally not measurable and help to provide a general framework for the course. Again, writing course and unit goals should start with a description of what you expect students to look like at the end of the course. Our own work describing our target undergraduate students led to these course goals:

> In today's information-rich world, the ability to use information effectively is essential to success in college and beyond. This course will help students become effective users of information by providing them with the background and skills necessary to locate, critically evaluate, and use information sources for specific purposes. In particular, students will be developing skills that they can use and apply in their college research papers.

Goals describe the course to students and inform them as to what they can expect to accomplish through their work in your course. However, students are often limited on time and will most likely scan a syllabus for the most important information and course goals are often overlooked. Thus, course goals should be kept to a minimum. We strive to include four to five broad goals in the syllabus and one or two goals per unit.

IL TOPICS IN AN ONLINE COURSE

Once you have a good idea of what you want your students to look like at the end of your course, you can start identifying possible course topics that you will later turn into course units or modules. A good place to start looking for topics is the ACRL Information Literacy Competency Standards, Performance Indicators, and Outcomes.[1] In addition to the ACRL Standards, you can use IL textbooks and other syllabi for more ideas. If you are developing a department-specific course, you will also need to look at the department's curriculum, course syllabi, and course assignments. The ACRL Information Literacy in the Disciplines wiki is useful for identifying discipline-specific IL learning objectives and teaching strategies.[2]

A list of the initial list of topics we brainstormed for our general information literacy undergraduate course are:

- Library catalog
- Library web site
- Databases: Academic Search Complete, JSTOR, LexisNexis Academic
- Searching effectively: Boolean, truncation, proximity techniques

- Web resources
- Citation styles: MLA, APA, Chicago
- In-text citations
- Online learning
- LMS
- Evaluating sources
- Plagiarism
- Copyright and Fair Use
- Reference resources/background information
- Topics and research questions
- Bias/critical reading
- Information overload
- Information society
- Social media
- Keywords
- Information life cycle
- Popular and scholarly sources
- Primary and secondary sources
- Physical library
- Getting help at the library
- Library services
- Subject guides

Other sources for ideas on course topics arc articles that analyze syllabi from library research courses. Paul Hrycaj's article categorizes course topics by ACRL Information Literacy Competency Standards from one hundred syllabi of introductory library courses that he found online.[3] Not surprisingly, there were many more syllabi topics related to ACRL Standard 2 (information access—database and web searching) than any of the other standards. A recent study sought to update Hrycaj's 2006 findings by analyzing one hundred library research course syllabi found through online searches and solicitations on library instruction listervs.[4] The authors found that contrary to information access being the number-one topic in the 2006 study, the number-one topic in the 2012 study was citing sources and giving attribution (ACRL Standard 5—Ethical and Legal Use of Information). The 2012 study reflects current concerns voiced in higher education as students turn to the web for their research needs but are not yet well educated in giving credit to their sources.

WILL IT WORK ONLINE?

The ACRL Standards were not developed with a particular course format in mind. Rather, they were developed to describe the different concepts and behaviors the information literate student should master. However, you will find that several Information Literacy Standards and Outcomes do not lend themselves to the online environment. Each semester that we teach a course, we spend time reflecting on what worked, what needs more attention, and where changes need to be made, and we have come to learn that certain units do not work well in the online environment. The following course topics, often taught in face-to-face courses, need more thoughtful preparation in order to give the students more direction and to save instructor time.

Formulating a Research Topic

Coming up with a good research question is often the first step to conducting research, and you want your students to search for information in the context of an authentic research question, and hopefully in the context of a research assignment for a course. However, we have found that teaching students how to formulate a research question online does not work well. Often undergraduate students need help in the form of a conversation with an instructor that involves a back-and-forth question-and-answer session to come up with a suitable research question. In the online environment, it can take several days and even weeks to have this conversation. Instead of having students come up with their own research question, we provide students with several research questions to choose from.

Evaluating Information Resources

Any IL course should devote time to teaching students how to evaluate an information source for their particular need. Ideally, students choose their own information sources to evaluate and comment on. However, when each student chooses his or her own topic, the instructor could easily have hundreds of different sources that they will then need to read and evaluate. Alternatively, when students are asked to choose from among a group of topics, the instructor can provide them with a set of sources they are already familiar with. Although this method requires more upfront time, it will save the instructor time as they will not have to search for and then read through different sources for each student.

Web Resources

Students will often indicate that they had formal instruction in evaluating web sites and they feel comfortable evaluating and selecting web sites. However, we have found that with undergraduate students the opposite is true. We recommend a unit on evaluating web sites in which students are presented with several sites of varying quality and a set of criteria they can use to analyze and evaluate those web sites. Again, having those sites already picked out for the students will save much grading time.

Citation Management

This topic has less to do with learning an IL concept and more about actually following a multistep process. It can be tedious to provide step-by-step instructions on how to export references from a specific database to RefWorks, create a folder, and then share the folder with the instructor. Our solution in the online course was to have students watch a RefWorks video on YouTube to get an overview of how RefWorks functions. We then provide instructions on how to export references from a database and the library catalog. We also refer them to a RefWorks video on sharing references with others. A combination of videos and written instructions compensates for not being able to help students individually when they get stuck. We also encourage students to use the library's chat reference service or to e-mail us when they need help.

COURSE UNITS: SCOPE AND SEQUENCE

Depending on the length of the course and the number of credit hours, you will most likely not have the time to teach everything you would like to, and it is better to start small and grow the curriculum as you develop the overall plan. As you decide which topics to keep and how to sequence them, keep in mind that to master a concept, a tool, or a strategy, a student must be given the appropriate time and activities to do so. Students will not learn how to use a database properly unless they are able to interact with it in a number of ways over time. Thus, one weekly unit can consist of several student activities including tutorials, assignments, quizzes, and discussions. Additionally, you will also need to make time for instructor activities including grading, responding to discussions, and fielding student questions. Course units should be sequenced so that they build and expand on each other and are not treated as isolated units. The appendices in this chapter include course units from the online courses we teach. These sample course modules were included for their breadth of topics and effective sequencing.

As you select, sequence, and develop course units, you will want to keep in mind how much time it will take students to complete a unit and how much "seat time" your institution requires to award a credit. The Carnegie Unit has long been the standard by which education institutions measure what a credit unit is. It is based on seat time with one credit unit being equivalent to one hour of in-class time and two hours of time spent on coursework outside of the class.[5] The Carnegie Unit has received much criticism since its adoption for its focus on seat time that measures how much time students spend in the class and not on what they know.[6] Additionally, in self-paced online courses, students will vary in how much time they spend on each unit. However, having a baseline of two or three hours per week per credit hour will help guide the development process and ensure that students are given approximately the same amount of work each week.

Once you have your units selected and sequenced, you should begin the work of writing learning goals for each unit. Remember to limit unit or module goals to just one or two. Once you have the general layout of the course along with unit goals, you can move on to deciding what you want your students to learn in each unit.

OUTCOMES: SPECIFIC AND MEASURABLE

The ACRL Standards include an exhaustive list of IL outcomes and performance indicators. However, you will most likely need to tailor them to fit your students' particular needs and your own teaching preferences and teaching philosophy. Additionally, these outcomes include a lot of library terminology that may not be familiar to students. Finally, if you do choose to use these outcomes instead of writing your own, you will need to adapt them to the online environment. For these reasons, we recommend writing your own outcomes and using the ACRL Standards as a guide.

Like goals, student learning outcomes should be focused on the student and the student's behavior. However, student learning outcomes differ from goals in two major ways: they are more specific and they are measurable. Outcomes that are specific and measurable should allow you to easily see what you will teach and how you will assess it. Compare these three student learning outcomes:

- Students will know how to use the library catalog.
- Students will understand the library catalog's search features.
- Students will list three of the library catalog's different search features.

In looking at these outcomes you should notice that all three outcomes are focused on the students and describe what the student should be able to do after a lesson. That is, each outcome begins with "the student will" followed by the behavior we expect to see in the student. However, the first outcome is too broad. Knowing how to use the library catalog involves a series of related tasks and procedures along with knowledge of specific terminology. It is also difficult to discern which areas of using the library catalog will be taught. Will accessing the catalog be taught? Or perhaps author searching or keyword searching? Broad outcomes are not helpful to students or instructors because instructors will not know exactly what they should be teaching and students will be lost as to what it is they should be learning. The second outcome is more specific in that it focuses on one aspect of the catalog—its search features—but how to assess a student's understanding of those features is not readily apparent. The third outcome is both more specific and measurable. With this outcome you have a clear understanding of what you need to teach, the different search options available in the catalog, and how you will assess the outcome, that is by asking the student to list three different types of search options available in the library catalog.

The key to writing outcomes that are both measurable and specific is to use action verbs. The first two examples use the verbs *know* and *understand* which are vague, passive, and difficult to measure. Other verbs you should avoid using when writing learning outcomes include *grasp*, *appreciate*, *learn*, *master*, *comprehend*, *notice*, and *experience*. Table 3.1 shows outcomes written with both passive and action verbs for the broad goal: *Students will successfully use the library catalog to fulfill a variety of information needs*.

The examples given in Table 3.1 center on knowledge-based outcomes that focus on what students should know. However, even if students *know* the catalog's URL, how books are arranged in the library, and what items can be searched in the catalog, they may not know how to use this knowledge. Additionally, because IL is composed of a set of skills and tasks and not just concepts, your student outcomes cannot solely focus on what students should know. Rather, your curriculum should include a variety of student learning outcomes from simple knowledge outcomes to more cognitively sophisticated outcomes such as application and evaluation. That is, outcomes should progressively move from what students should know to what students should be able to do with that knowledge.

Table 3.1.   Passive and Active Learning Outcomes

Passive Verb Outcomes	Action Verb Outcomes
Students will know which items are included in the library catalog.	Students will list items that are available in the library catalog.
Students will know the correct URL for the library catalog.	Students will identify the correct URL for the library catalog.
Students will understand how books are arranged in the library.	Students will describe how books are arranged in the library.
Students will know how to read a catalog record.	Students will label different parts of a catalog record.

An understanding of Bloom's Taxonomy can help greatly in writing student learning outcomes that build on each other and address different types of student behaviors. Developed in the 1950s by a team of educators led by Benjamin Bloom, the taxonomy is a hierarchical list of six categories of objectives (knowledge, comprehension, application, analysis, synthesis, and evaluation) that fall under the cognitive domain.[7]

The categories were revised in 2001 to reflect more current research into cognitive psychology and include two dimensions: a cognitive and a knowledge dimension.[8] The new knowledge dimension includes four types of knowledge: factual, conceptual, procedural, and metacognitive. Like the original taxonomy, the updated version is hierarchical with the last category, create, representing higher order thinking skills than the previous category. Iowa State University has an interactive model of the taxonomy that shows how the two dimensions work together.[9] The categories for the cognitive dimension are summarized and listed here and have been adapted from Krathwol.[10]

1. Remember:
    a. Recognizing
    b. Recalling
2. Understand:
    a. Interpreting
    b. Exemplifying
    c. Classifying
    d. Summarizing
    e. Inferring
    f. Comparing
    g. Explaining
3. Apply:
    a. Executing
    b. Implementing
4. Analyze:
    a. Differentiating
    b. Organizing
    c. Attributing
5. Evaluate:
    a. Checking
    b. Critiquing
6. Create:
    a. Generating
    b. Planning
    c. Producing

Table 3.2.   Outcomes Aligned with Bloom's Taxonomy

Remember	Students will describe the characteristics of a scholarly source.
Understand	Students will explain the differences between scholarly and popular sources.
Apply	When shown different sources of information, students will classify them as popular or scholarly.
Analyze	Students will distinguish popular sources from scholarly ones.
Evaluate	Students will determine when to use both popular and scholarly sources in a paper to support their own argument.
Create	Students will create a bibliography that includes both popular and scholarly sources.

Table 3.2 shows a range of progressively more sophisticated outcomes for the broad goal, *Students will understand and use popular and scholarly sources.*

The revised Bloom's Taxonomy also includes alternative names, or action verbs, for the different categories.[11] Bloom's Taxonomy is most useful when it is used along with these action verbs as shown in Table 3.3. These action verbs can help greatly with writing outcomes and developing test items. This table was adapted from the action verbs used in Mastascusa, et al.[12] Examples of learning outcomes that use these action verbs for our graduate and undergraduate online courses can be seen in resources for this chapter.

Table 3.3. Bloom's Taxonomy and Action Verbs

Remember	arrange, define, describe, duplicate, identify, label, list, match, name, order, outline, recognize, recall, repeat, reproduce, select, state
Understand	classify, convert, defend, discuss, distinguish, estimate, explain, express, extend, generalize, give examples, identify, indicate, infer, locate, paraphrase, predict, recognize, rewrite, report, restate, review, select, summarize, translate
Apply	apply, change, choose, demonstrate, discover, dramatize, employ, illustrate, interpret, manipulate, modify, operate, practice, predict, prepare, produce, relate schedule, show, sketch, solve, use
Analyze	analyze, appraise, breakdown, categorize, compare, contrast, criticize, diagram, differentiate, discriminate, distinguish, examine, experiment, identify, illustrate, infer, model, outline, point out, question, relate, select, separate, subdivide
Evaluate	appraise, argue, assess, attach, choose, compare, conclude, contrast, defend, describe, discriminate, estimate, valuate, explain, judge, justify, interpret, relate, predict, rate, select, summarize, support, value
Create	arrange, assemble, categorize, collect, combine, comply, compose, construct, create, design, develop, devise, explain, formulate, generate, plan, prepare, propose, rearrange, reconstruct, relate, reorganize, revise, rewrite, summarize, synthesize

TEXTBOOKS

There are several advantages to using a textbook in your online course. A well-chosen textbook offers opportunities for more in-depth exploration of a concept than what can be presented in slides, video lectures, or podcasts. A textbook can also provide ready-made assignments, assessments, and illustrations to save preparation time. Using a textbook can provide consistency in course content where there are a number of instructors teaching the course. It is also a great way to get new instructors up-to-speed on course content.[13]

On the other hand, online learning lends itself to participatory and personal exploration of the concepts introduced in the course, rather than a content-focused approach that can rely on passively reading a chapter from a textbook.[14] Additionally, a textbook may not offer students a variety of perspectives found in readings from several authors. A textbook provides only one modality for learning. With technology, a student can move through a tutorial to explore the functionality of a database such as JSTOR and answer questions and receive responses along the way to keep them on track. They can view videos of researchers and graduate students talking about benefits of open access to scholarly literature and author's rights. To provide up-to-date information, it is easier and certainly more cost-effective for instructors to adopt new readings and tutorials as they become available, rather than have students pay a considerable amount of money for a new textbook.

However, if the decision is made to use a textbook or chapters of a textbook, there are a number of considerations to make:

1. Requiring students to purchase a textbook is not as onerous for distance students as it once was because many textbooks are now available online from the campus bookstore or through an online book vendor at a discounted price.
2. Determine if your institution is supporting e-textbooks through an e-textbook publisher or platform.
3. Find out if the library can provide a multi-user license for the e-textbook.
4. Explore open education resources (OER) sites for free or inexpensive e-textbooks.
5. Link to scanned chapters of a textbook while adhering to copyright laws and fair use guidelines.

New IL textbooks for students are constantly being added to the marketplace. The ACRL Instruction Section Teaching Methods Committee has a web site for an up-to-date listing of library instruction textbooks with brief annotations and references to published reviews.[15]

KNOW THIS . . .

- Developing an effective curriculum takes a great deal of thinking about student needs, course goals, learning outcomes, course topics, sequencing units, and deciding whether or not to use a textbook.
- Ask yourself what you already know about your students and their information literacy learning needs.
- To gain a better understanding of what your course goals should be, create a persona of a student that describes them after taking your course.
- Look for course topics in library research instruction textbooks, the ACRL Standards, and library syllabi available on the web.
- Use action verbs to write specific and measurable learning outcomes.
- When writing outcomes, focus on what you want your students to be able to do and not so much on what you want them to know.
- Some information literacy topics and assignments do not work well in an asynchronous online environment. Think about how you might make these assignments more manageable for you and your students.
- Course curriculum that encourages active participation and application of learning may not lend itself to using a textbook.

APPENDIX 1

Resource 3.1
Sample Undergraduate Course Topics and Learning Outcomes

LIBR197R—The Online Research Lab

Week 1: Introduction to the Online Research Lab
Students will be able to:
- Navigate D2L successfully
- Identify strategies for online learning
- Describe the main focus of this course
- Describe different information resources
- Define information and information overload and how it effects individuals

Week 2: Background Information
Students will be able to:
- Locate one encyclopedia source related to their topic

- Locate one article in the database CQ Researcher
- Locate one background article
- Describe major themes, issues, and definitions related to their topic
- Identify the major parts of an MLA citation

Week 3: Media Bias
Students will be able to:
- Describe two opposing viewpoints related to their topic
- Identify types of bias in an article

Week 4: Popular and Scholarly Sources
Students will be able to:
- Describe popular and scholarly sources
- Differentiate between popular and scholarly sources
- Identify scholarly articles for their research question

Week 5: Evaluating Web Resources
Students will be able to:
- Assess the reliability of different sources of information
- Explain why the Web and Google are not the best information sources for college papers
- Distinguish reliable sites from those that are less reliable
- List a set of criteria on which to evaluate web sites critically

Week 6: Using the UA Library Catalog
Students will be able to:
- Use the UA Library Catalog to conduct a search and locate a book
- Access and retrieve a book in different formats
- Use parts of a citation to retrieve a book
- Evaluate the usefulness of books in different formats
- Describe how new technologies are replacing print materials

Week 7: Searching Effectively
Students will be able to:
- Distinguish between effective and poor search strings
- Create effective search strings
- Describe Academic Search Complete and its features
- Use Academic Search Complete to locate different information sources
- Identify the different parts of a citation
- Use a citation to locate an article using the UA Library Catalog

Week 8: Using Additional Databases
Students will be able to:
- List characteristics of JSTOR
- List characteristics of LexisNexis Academic
- Use JSTOR to complete several tasks including how to locate material
- Use LexisNexis to complete several tasks including how to locate material
- Compare and contrast the content of different databases
- Compare and contrast the features of different databases

Week 9: Avoiding Plagiarism
Students will be able to:
- Define plagiarism
- Evaluate scenarios for possible plagiarism
- Compose correctly formatted citations

APPENDIX 2

Resource 3.2
Sample Graduate Course Topics and Learning Outcomes

LIBR 696a—Information Research Strategies for Graduates Students and Researchers

Week 1
Module 1: Introduction to the Course
Students will be able to:
- Describe the course content
- Explain how to get help from the instructors and other students
- Summarize the purpose and deadlines for components of the research portfolio

Module 2: The Information Search Process
Students will be able to:
- Identify the stages in the information search process as described by Carol Kuhlthau
- Reflect on their thoughts, feelings, actions, and strategies that accompany each stage of the information search process

Week 2
Module 1: Effective Search Strategies
Students will be able to:
- Demonstrate effective database searching techniques, including use of Boolean operators and truncation
- Successfully locate relevant citations and full text sources from Academic Search
- Store saved searches, search results, and an alert for new articles using MyEbscoHost
- Successfully locate relevant records in the UA Library Catalog
- Store a search statement using the "Preferred Searches" feature in the UA Library catalog to receive notification of new materials on that topic

Module 2: Setting up the Research Portfolio Framework
Students will be able to:
- Create a web site for their research portfolio
- Add biographical introductory content from Week 1 to their web site following the requirements outlined in this module
- Share their portfolio web site with the instructor

Week 3: Citation Management
Students will be able to:
- Import citations from databases into a citation management program
- Create a folder in a citation management program
- Create a formatted bibliography using a citation management program
- Share a folder from a citation management program

Week 4: Disciplinary Databases
Students will be able to:
- Identify library databases related to their discipline
- Locate and use database tutorials and help files to improve search effectiveness
- Describe key features and functions of discipline-specific library databases
- Export references from disciplinary databases into a citation management tool

Week 5: Multidisciplinary Databases
Students will be able to:
- Effectively search JSTOR, WorldCat Local, Google Scholar and Web of Science to retrieve appropriate research articles

- Import references into a citation management program from JSTOR, WorldCat Local, Google Scholar, and Web of Science
- Conduct a cited reference search in Web of Science to locate related articles

Week 6:
Module 1: Introduction to the Literature Review
Students will be able to:
- Describe different types of literature reviews and which type of literature review format is most relevant for their thesis or dissertation
- Summarize the components and characteristics of a good literature review
- Describe criteria for evaluating the completeness of a literature review

Module 2: Dissertations and Theses
Students will be able to:
- Identify databases that can be used to find dissertations and theses
- Search effectively to locate both UA and non-UA dissertations and theses
- Locate full-text online or print copies of dissertations and theses

Week 7: Scholarly Communication and Open Access
Students will be able to:
- Articulate key issues regarding the open access movement within the arena of scholarly communication
- Describe open access publishing options for scholarly communication in their discipline

Week 8: Copyright and Fair Use
Students will be able to:
- Explain basic principles of the U.S. Copyright Laws
- Explain the basic principles of the Fair Use section of the U.S. Copyright Laws (17 U.S.C. Section 107)
- Apply principles of the U.S. Copyright Laws and Fair Use to the academic and research setting

Week 9: Social Media and Scholarly Networking
Students will be able to:
- Identify social networking and collaboration tools which are useful for scholarly/academic purposes
- Describe the positive and negative implications of social media for scholarly networking

Week 10: End of Course Reflection
Students will be able to:
- Reflect on course learning in relation to the course goals and learning objectives

NOTES

1. Association of College & Research Libraries, *Information Literacy Competency Standards for Higher Education.* (Chicago, IL : American Library Association, 2000).
2. ACRL Instruction Section. "Information Literacy in the Disciplines," http://wikis.ala.org/acrl/index.php/Information_literacy_in_the_disciplines.
3. Paul L. Hrycaj, "An Analysis of Online Syllabi for Credit-Bearing Library Skills Courses," *College & Research Libraries* 67, no. 6 (2006): 525–535.
4. Rachael E. Elrod, Elise D. Wallace, and Cecelia B. Sirigos, "Teaching Information Literacy: A Review of 100 Syllabi," *The Southeastern Librarian* 60, no. 3 (2012): 4.
5. Dan Berrett, "Carnegie Teaching Foundation, Inventor of the Credit Hour, Seeks to Change It." *Chronicle Of Higher Education* 59, no. 16 (2012): A25. EBSCOhost Academic Search Complete.
6. Jennifer Patterson Lorenzetti, "Time Up for the Credit Hour?" *Distance Education Report* 17, no. 5 (March 1, 2013): 1–8.
7. Benjamin S. Bloom, ed., *Taxonomy of Educational Objectives: The Classification of Educational Goals. Handbook I: Cognitive Domain* (New York: Longmans, Green, 1956).
8. David R. Krathwohl, "A Revision of Bloom's Taxonomy: An Overview," *Theory into Practice* 41, no. 4 (2002): 212–218; Thomas J. Lasley, "Bloom's Taxonomy," in *Encyclopedia of Educational Reform and Dissent*, James C. Carper, et al., eds., (Thousand Oaks, CA: SAGE Publications, Inc., 2010): 107–110.
9. Iowa State University. Center for Excellence in Learning and Teaching. "A Model of Learning Objectives Based on 'A Taxonomy for Learning, Teaching, and Assessing: A Revision of Bloom's Taxonomy of Educational Objectives,'" ISU. Center for Excellence in Learning and Teaching, 2012, available at http://www.celt.iastate.edu/pdfs-docs/teaching/RevisedBloomsHandout.pdf, accessed on January 15, 2014.
10. David R. Krathwohl, "A Revision of Bloom's Taxonomy."
11. Lorin W. Anderson, et al., *A Taxonomy for Learning, Teaching, and Assessing: A Revision of Bloom's Taxonomy of Educational Objectives*, L. W. Anderson and D. R. Krathwohl, eds. (New York, London: Addison Wesley, Longmann, 2001).
12. Edward J. Mastascusa, William J. Snyder, and Brian S. Hoyt, *Effective Instruction for STEM Discipline: From Learning Theory to College Teaching* (San Francisco: Jossey-Bass, 2011): 221–232.
13. Rochelle Rodrigo, "Why We Won't See Textbooks in Our Disciplinary Rear View Mirrors in the Near Future," *Teaching English in the Two-Year College*, 39, no. 3, (March 2012): 309–311.

14. Barbara Wittkopf, "Recreating the Credit Course in an Online Environment Issues and Concerns," *Reference & User Services Quarterly* 43, no. 1 (Fall 2003): 18–25.

15. ACRL Instruction Section. Teaching Methods Committee. "Textbooks for Students," available at http://www.ala.org/acrl/aboutacrl/directoryofleadership/sections/is/iswebsite/projpubs/textbooksstudents, accessed on January 15, 2014.

Chapter Four

Creating a Student-Centered Syllabus: Taking It to the Next Level

Many aspects of online courses look quite different from their face-to-face counterpart, and the syllabus is no different. At its core, the primary function of a syllabus has not changed significantly: it still provides students with a description of the course, course policies, and a schedule of topics and assignments, and it is still a crucial part of a course associated with excellent instruction.[1] However, today's syllabus can be easily transformed into a colorful, hypertext web page full of audio and video clips, images, and links. Thus, what was once a long, mundane, text-heavy document distributed on the first day of classes and sporadically consulted throughout the semester has turned into a dynamic and interactive learning object.

In this chapter we begin by addressing the importance of the syllabus and the roles it plays in the course for both the student and the instructor. We then delineate essential syllabi components. The chapter finishes with an exploration of how to create syllabi using multimedia technologies that are more engaging and readily used by students. Sample syllabi from our undergraduate and graduate courses are provided in the appendices.

WHAT IS A SYLLABUS GOOD FOR ANYWAY?

Sinor and Kaplan describe a syllabus as both an end product, the culmination of your course planning, and a beginning, an introduction to the course for your students.[2] The syllabus does indeed play these two roles and many others. Traditionally, the syllabus' main function is to provide students with information about the course including a schedule of important dates and course topics, a list of materials that will be used in the course, a series of policies, and information on contacting you, the instructor. The traditional syllabus can also be viewed as a contract between you and your students. It is an agreed-on list of assignments, due dates, and rules and responsibilities that everyone involved in the course, including the instructor, is expected to follow. Because of this contractual nature, making any critical changes to the syllabus once the course has started is unfair to the students.[3] In contrast to a traditional syllabus, a learner-centered syllabus "reinforces the intentions, roles, attitudes, and strategies that you will use to promote active, purposeful, and effective learning."[4] Essentially, a learner-centered syllabus becomes an instructional tool critical to students' success.

In the online environment, the syllabus' functionality as a roadmap is critical because the LMS can be a confusing place for students, especially the first time they log in to a course. In terms of "getting lost" on the first day of class, the LMS can be just as difficult to navigate as a large university campus. Students repeatedly tell us that they cannot find items in the LMS even when they are clearly labeled. As a roadmap, the syllabus provides students with information on how to get started and how to proceed through the course. It provides them with information on where to find content in the LMS, how the course works, where to get help, and it makes students aware of important submission dates. The syllabus as a roadmap allows students to see the "big picture" by emphasizing the relationship between the course goals, activities and tasks, and how their learning and participation will be assessed. The use of graphics and hyperlinks within the syllabus makes these relationships more readily accessible and easier to comprehend.

Communicating your personality and the tone of the course is an important part of engaging students on the first day of class, but doing so in the online environment is much more difficult. The syllabus is often the first thing students in an online course will see; as such it can help in getting across your personality and setting the tone for the course. Including your teaching philosophy in your syllabus can also serve to communicate how you view and value learning.[5] The syllabus is also an ideal place to communicate your views on expected interactions with students. Online courses can seem impersonal and student evaluations often show that students wish for more communication and interactions with their instructors. Sinor and Kaplan suggest using the syllabus to help communicate your teaching style by writing it in the first person for an informal tone and in the third person for a more formal teaching style.[6] If using video, you can also use different levels of formality to set the tone for the course.

ELEMENTS OF THE COURSE SYLLABUS

Your syllabus will vary depending on your own preferences and what your department or institution requires you to include. However, the following elements are needed to ensure a quality, student-centered syllabus.

- Course Title: Include identifying course information, such as course number, section, credit hours, and start and end dates.
- Course Description: The clarity and tone of the course description can make all the difference in setting a positive and enthusiastic response to the course curriculum. Use language that will make students curious to read and interact with the entire syllabus.[7] The language in the course description should also get students excited about taking the course and succeeding in it.
- Instructor Contact Information: In this section you should include your name, campus address, phone number, fax, e-mail address, and office hours. In addition to providing this basic information, you could also add a brief description of your teaching philosophy and your teaching background.
- Communication with the Instructor: Let students know your communication preferences. Fully describe the time frame students can expect to get their questions answered. Explain how often you will be visiting the course site, such as, twice a day or three days during the week. List the days and times you will be available to answer their questions. For example, "I am available from 9:30 AM to 7:30 PM PST Mon–Fri." Make the days and times explicit because you may have students from different time zones.

  Include directions for how students should address e-mail messages to you. We often receive e-mails with no subject, no student name, or no content, so we now include directions on how to format e-mails in our syllabus. If you plan on using any external social networking sites such as Twitter, Facebook, or a wiki, provide students with the links and directions for setting up accounts.
- Student Behavior: Although you will not need to include expectations for student behavior in the classroom, students will be interacting with each other and should be made aware of expected behavior concerning discussions with other students. In our courses, we remind students of the importance of respecting other's opinions, and let them know that we will not tolerate flaming, profanity, and other aggressive online behavior.
- Course Goals and Learning Outcomes: Overall course goals and learning outcomes are important to include in your syllabus so that students know exactly what they will be learning. One educator suggests adding a disclaimer that if students follow the course policies, make a good effort in

the assignments, complete tests, and take part in discussions, that they will achieve the learning outcomes outlined in the course.[8]

- Required Course Texts, Learning Materials, and Software: If you are using a course text, include information about how students can purchase a copy. Explain that reading material can be downloaded from the course site and include information on required word processing/viewing software, such as Word or Adobe Reader for viewing PDF documents for assignments or readings. If there are Adobe Flash tutorials, provide information on how students can download the latest version of the Adobe Flash player to their computer. For synchronous online conferencing, podcasts, and videocasts, include information about how to locate downloads for these software programs.

- Technology Support: Include contact information for the LMS technology support staff, hours of availability and any help pages or FAQs for the LMS. If you plan to use a citation management program, include links to online help information.

- Library Assistance: Provide information on how to contact the library's reference and information desks. Linking to the library's chat reference service lets students know that there is assistance with their questions when you, the instructor are not available.

- Writing Help: If your course has writing assignments, provide information on support from your writing center. During our online graduate student course, we also make announcements about graduate student writing workshops.

- How the Course Works: Provide students with an overview of when course units will be released, when assignments are due, how to use the LMS functionality to submit assignments, participate in discussions, and check their progress through the grade book.

- Participation Expectations: Let students know that active participation is an important element of the course and they will be graded on participation in discussions, both in the quantity and the quality of their responses. Include expectations about the number of times per week that students need to log in to the course site for new announcements and discussion postings. LMS analytics functionality make it is easy to see how many times and for how long a student has logged into the course and accessed different course units.

- Course Schedule: Present the course schedule by weeks or units. Include topics, readings, discussions, tests and quizzes, assignments, and due dates for assignments. For our online courses, we present the course schedule in the syllabus as well as a weekly topic outline and due dates on the course home page, so that students can readily view the overall flow of the course units and weekly deadlines.

- Grades: Your grading scheme reflects what you want students to learn and where they should focus their time.[9] It should align with course goals, learning outcomes, and assignments and be clearly communicated to students. Consider providing a rationale for your grading system so that students have a clear understanding of what you are grading and why you think it is important as a measurement of student learning. Your grading system should be consistent throughout the course and should not be changed without careful consideration of the consequences and giving a clear rationale for the change to students.[10]

Grading components should be made up of a variety of learning assessment activities such as assignments, presentations, discussions, quizzes, and final projects. This not only varies the types of assessments, but it also takes into consideration different learning preferences and provides students with a variety of opportunities to demonstrate their understanding of the content in a holistic manner.[11]

Review your institution's grading policies to determine what grading system is used and what constitutes an Incomplete or Withdraw grade. Link to the institution's grading policies in your syllabus as a resource for students to gain a broader understanding of your grading scheme.

Here is a common grading system:

A = 90–100% Excellent

B = 80–89% Good/Above Average

C = 70–79% Satisfactory/Average

D = 60–69% Poor/Below Average

F = 0–59% Failure/Unsatisfactory

I = Incomplete

W = Withdraw (approved withdrawal from the course)

There is also the Pass/Fail option, in which a Pass for the course is equivalent to a D or better. Check your institution's grading policy for regulations on the use of Pass/Fail for undergraduate and graduate courses. For our courses, we have chosen not to offer the P/F option because we have found that students are not fully engaged with the learning materials and assignments when they have the P/F option.

Another issue to consider is allowing a student to audit your course. If you do so, determine the level of participation you expect from an auditing student. If a student is not participating at the agreed-on level, then you have the option to administratively drop the student. Again check your institution's grading policies for guidelines.

- Course Grading Approaches: You will also need to decide which grading method to use. You can choose to use a criterion based method where students' grades represent their individual achievement or a "normed" based method in which only a certain percentage of students receive an A grade, whereas the majority of students receive a C and a few students receive a D.[12] This is often referred to as grading on a curve, in which students are graded in relation to other students in the course. We recommend using the criterion-based grading method so that students are assessed on their individual achievements and not in relation to other students' achievements.

  There are two common approaches to calculating course grades. In a weighted grading system, the grading components are given a weight represented as a percentage of the entire grade.[13] For example, using a weighted grading approach, a research project might have a weight of 45 percent of the total grade; quizzes 10 percent; assignments 35 percent; and discussions a weight of 10 percent. In this scenario, students clearly know that if they want a good grade, they should spend most of their effort on the research project and the assignments. In the weighted grading approach, each item in a grading component must add up to the assigned weighted number of points. To make this easier, you can assign each item within a grading component an equal number of points.

  In a points system, what is important is the accumulation of points from all grading components. If a student does poorly in one area, it is possible to accumulate enough points in another area to make up the deficit.[14] In this case, the final course grades would be determined by calculating percentages of the total accumulated points. For example, if the total possible number of points is 500, and a letter grade A is equivalent to 90–100 percent of the total number of points, then the points calculation for an A is $90–100 \times 500 = 450–500$ points. If you are using an LMS, the grade book is able to accommodate both types of grading systems.

- Grading Policies: In addition to a full and detailed explanation of how points will be assigned and how grades will be calculated, you also need to include a detailed explanation of assignment expectations, late or missed assignments, absences, and extra credit.

- Assignment expectations: Students should be made aware of the procedure for submitting assignments and general requirements for how assignments will be graded. Let students know if you want them to e-mail assignments directly to you or if they should upload them to the LMS and be consistent. In either case, you should provide explicit directions on how to send or upload assignments and how to title saved assignments. You should also let students know how to format assignments and if any points will be taken off for incorrect formatting, uploading, or saving. In this section, also include expectations for grammar, usage, spelling, and overall professionalism in assignments.

- Late assignments: If you accept late assignments, you need to let students know under what conditions you will accept late assignments and how many, if any, points will be deducted from the total points. When we told our undergraduate students that they would lose five points for every day an assignment was late, we found that we received many more late assignments compared to when we adopted a "no late assignments" policy. In this case, we only accept late assignments in extreme cases with prior notice. Having fewer late papers has made grading and general course management much easier for us.
- Absences: Absences are generally not a concern in asynchronous courses. If you plan on offering any type of synchronous components such as web conferencing as part of the course, you should let students know if they are mandatory or elective. If mandatory, let students know the consequences of not attending a web conference. For synchronous courses, you should let students know of your attendance policy, how attendance will be taken, and if students will lose points for not attending the synchronous portions of the course.
- Extra credit: If you offer extra-credit work, let students know what the extra-credit work will consist of, when it can be submitted, and how many points are possible.
- Other Standard Policies: Your institution will likely have requirements mandating specific policies and wording that must be included in your syllabus. These policies should include the following:
  - Accommodations for students with special needs
  - Academic integrity
  - Confidentiality of student records
  - Religious observations
  - Administrative drops
- Schedule-May-Change Disclaimer: As noted, the syllabus should be treated as a contract between you and your students and should not change significantly over the length of the course. However, it is possible that some modifications may need to be made to the syllabus, and students should be made aware of this. In our courses we include wording that indicates that the syllabus is subject to change with advanced notice from the instructor.
- Other Topics to Include: In addition to these suggested topics for inclusion in the syllabus, we have compiled a list of less common topics you may want to include in your syllabus:[15]
  - Teaching philosophy
  - Support services information

- Tutoring centers
- Counseling centers
- Group project guidelines
- Time required for course success
- Nonrequired related readings, web sites, and videos
- Study strategies including information on how to succeed in an online course
- Time management skills
- Sample typical errors made by students
- Sample test questions

THE INTERACTIVE SYLLABUS

To today's technologically savvy students who are accustomed to multimedia presentations of information, the long, text-based syllabus will seem like a relic abandoned with the chalkboard. Fortunately, the online course allows you to provide your students with an immersive and interactive syllabus that is dynamic and robust and quite different from the syllabus of years past. Richards describes the interactive syllabus as one that has a "high level of initial interaction between the learner and the material, resulting in increasingly progressive engagement with course materials."[16] As described by Richards, the interactive syllabus goes beyond the functions of the traditional syllabus and acts as both a container and access point for the course content.[17] Because of these additional functions, Windham uses the term *assignment guide* instead of syllabus.[18] Thus, the interactive syllabus has two functions: syllabus and assignment guide. In this chapter we discuss the first function, that of the syllabus, and in chapter 5 we present the assignment guide as a component of course content beyond the syllabus.

In the online environment, the dynamic, multimedia syllabus does far more than the text-based syllabus, but still keeps the traditional functions of the text-based syllabus. Figures 4.1 and 4.2 show many of the different features that help to create an effective interactive syllabus.

We offer the following suggestions for developing a creative and student-centered interactive syllabus:

- Video and Audio: Video can be used to introduce yourself and the course to the student. A video introduction is beneficial in that it is more personal and will appeal to different learning styles. Alternatively, you can include short audio clips or a podcast to introduce the course or to put greater emphasis on specific areas of the syllabus that you want to highlight. You can also embed

Use ↑ to navigate

Welcome to the Online Research Lab

If you regularly use Wikipedia or Google to locate information
for your research papers, then this course is for you. In this
papers. This course will take you through the basics of
conducting research with resources from the University of
Arizona Library.

YOUR INSTRUCTOR

Figure 4.1. Interactive Syllabus for an Information Literacy Course

video links to sites such as YouTube where your institution or library may already have videos welcoming students to the campus or introducing them to different services. You can also create a screencast video as part of the syllabus that introduces students to the LMS.

- Images: A basic best practice of online instruction is to use images for visual learning where needed and not for purely decorative reasons. This may be more difficult in the syllabus, but images can be used to introduce yourself, to show students particular buildings, the campus, the library, or just to break up text to make it more readable. We also use images including comic strips and quotes to break the syllabus up for students.
- Links: Links can be used in a number of ways including reducing superfluous text by linking to pages with the same or more information. For example, you do not need to include all of the information related to the institution's student code of conduct, but you can include links to specific areas of the code that you want students to have ready access to. You can also include direct links to useful campus resources such as the writing center, your e-mail, and the LMS help pages.
- Menus: Instead of presenting the syllabus as one long web page that students must scroll through to get the information they need, use sidebar

Figure 4.2. Interactive Syllabus for an Emerging Media Course

menus and linked chapter headings that allow students to navigate the syllabus at their own pace and as they need it. Figure 4.2 shows an interactive syllabus menu.

- Comprehension Checks: Easy to use instruction-based HTML editors such as SoftChalk allow for the development of pages with not only links and images but also with quiz questions. You can quickly insert multiple choice questions to keep students on track and allow them to check their understanding of the material.
- Course Schedule: The course schedule is an integral component of any syllabus and the one section students routinely check. With an interactive syllabus, you can make it easier for students to access material by including links from course topics to readings, activities, assignments, quizzes, and other course materials.

As a counterpoint to our enthusiasm for interactive syllabi, we should point out that the traditional text-based syllabus needs to be included in an online course for students who need special accommodations for accessing and reading the syllabus. Often dynamic, multimedia web pages are problematic for assistive software such as screen readers, so we include a formatted Word or PDF document in all of our courses.

WILL THEY USE IT?

A syllabus can reduce student anxiety by providing them with a clearly written description of what they will be learning, how they will demonstrate learning, and how they will be assessed.[19] But do students use the syllabus as often as they should? The common perception among faculty seems to be that students ignore the syllabus or misplace it at some point during the course.[20] Lack of use can be attributed to syllabi that are excessively long, contain typical "cookie cutter" information students have repeatedly seen in other courses, and include information they can get elsewhere in the LMS more easily.[21] Armstrong notes that text-heavy syllabi do not take into consideration different learning styles or the needs of non-native English speakers.[22] However, contrary to faculty perceptions that syllabi are often ignored by students, Calhoon and Becker found that the majority of students do use their syllabus throughout a course.[23] They also found that students tend to consult a syllabus when it was more detailed and included more information concerning homework assignments.[24] Thus, for students to use the syllabus as a tool for learning, it should include detailed information that students will need in order to complete course assignments each week.

However, even the best and most comprehensive syllabus can be ignored or forgotten by students. In addition to creating a clearly written and detailed syllabus, you will need to develop other strategies to ensure that students are aware of the syllabus content. In our undergraduate course, we have students complete a fun "Who Wants to Be a Millionaire" style game that asks students questions from the syllabus. As students answer questions correctly, they "win" more money until they reach the million dollar mark. Through the game we are able to highlight important areas in the syllabus, and students are able to self-assess their comprehension of it.

Reminding students of the syllabus at key points during the semester can also help in getting them to use it more frequently. Calhoon and Becker suggest reminding students of plagiarism or late-work policies referred to in the syllabus a week before an assignment is due.[25] Other suggested strategies include direct instruction in using the syllabus (this would work better with new undergraduate students) and surveying students on their use of the syllabus during the course.[26]

KNOW THIS . . .

- The student-centered, interactive syllabus is not only a reference for students but is also an integral part of the course.
- The syllabus is a road map to your course and should be created deliberately to set the expectations for the course.
- You can use the syllabus to communicate the tone of the course and your personality to the students.
- The syllabus has many functions including acting as a contract between the instructor and the student.
- Using video and audio in the syllabus allows you to make the course more personable and more engaging for students with different learning styles.
- The more detailed and informative a syllabus is, the more students will use it.
- Contrary to common faculty perceptions, students hold on to and consult their syllabus throughout the course.
- Online course instructors can create dynamic, multimedia syllabi that are robust and appealing.
- You should remind students about important deadlines and policies in the syllabus throughout the course.
- Most institutions offer helpful resources including syllabi templates that can help you create your syllabus more easily.

APPENDIX 1

Resource 4.1
Sample Syllabus Undergraduate Information Literacy Course

LIBR 197R—Online Research Lab
Spring 2013 Syllabus

Library Instructor: Jane Smith   **Office:** Main Library, Room A204
E-mail: jsmith@email.edu   **In-Office Hours:** Wednesdays 10 AM–11 AM
Phone: (XXX) 626–XXXX   **Online Office Hours:** Thursdays 10 AM–11 AM

NOTE: This lab begins on January 22, 2013

Lab Web Site
The Online Research Lab (ORL) is offered <u>ENTIRELY ONLINE</u> through D2L. Go to http://d2l.arizona.edu and log in (UA Net ID) to access the course site.

Required Texts:
There are no required texts for this class. Individual readings will be assigned and will be made available on D2L.

Other Required Materials:
- A UA Net ID account and access to the Internet
- Internet browser that supports D2L
- The latest version of Adobe Flash Player (free at http://get.adobe.com/flashplayer/)
- Flash drive (to save your work)

Lab Description
In today's information-rich world, the ability to use information effectively is essential to success in college and beyond. This course will help students become effective users of information by providing them with the background and skills necessary to locate, critically evaluate, and use information sources for specific purposes. In particular, students will be developing skills that they can use and apply in their college research papers.

Course Objectives and Expected Learning Outcomes
On completion of this course, students will be able to:
- Critically read and evaluate a wide array of information sources

- Determine the quality of an information source
- Create effective search strategies based on a chosen topic or research question
- Describe different sources of information and how they can satisfy different information needs
- Select and access an appropriate library source for an information need
- Effectively use different information sources including library catalogs, databases, and web search engines
- Use information sources in a manner that does not violate ethical standards
- Describe issues of information overload in society today

Participation/Attendance

Taking an online course can be quite different from taking a traditional course. To get the most out of this course you should **log in at least three times a week** instead of completing an entire unit in one sitting. This course has videos and tutorials that act like lectures in a regular class setting. You should plan on viewing materials on different days. You should also set aside specific study times so that you don't leave things until the last moment.

Navigating D2L

When using D2L for this class, the following information is recommended:
- Web site: http://www.d2l.arizona.edu
- D2L student tip sheet: http://help.d2l.arizona.edu/students/tip_sheet
- D2L Help pages: http://help.d2l.arizona.edu
- D2L often experiences service interruptions. If D2L goes down, your instructor will modify course dates and deadlines as needed and post changes to the course homepage.

DropBox

You will be asked to submit several assignments via the dropbox in D2L. All assignments should be saved with an extension **.doc** or **.docx** on your computer or flash drive. You must include your last name, first name, and the title of the assignment. Example: **SmithJohnAssignment1.docx**. To submit an assignment, click **Dropbox** > **Assignment** > **Add a File** > **Browse**. Next, select the file and click **Upload**, then click **Submit**.

Each time you submit an assignment to the dropbox, you will receive an e-mail verification from D2L; if an assignment has been incorrectly uploaded, you will not receive the e-mail verification. Any difficulties with the dropbox should be directed to d2l@email.arizona.edu.

Communication with Instructor

Emails:
When writing emails please do the following
- ○ **Subject Line:** Course title
- ○ **Body:** Include your first and last name

Students must allow instructor twenty-four (24) hours to respond to e-mails during the week and forty-eight (48) hours during the weekend.

In-Office Hours
Students are welcome to come by my office 10:00 to 11:00 AM on Wednesdays or else set up an appointment.

Online Office Hours
From 10:00 to 11:00 AM on Thursdays I will be available to chat in an Online Room on D2L. From the D2L toolbar, click **Online Rooms,** and then click the name of the room you'd like to virtually enter. Example: **Online Office Hours Week 3.**

Lab Schedule

With the exception of the first week, which begins on Tuesday, each unit will open on Monday at 8:00 AM. **All required work for the week will always be due on Sunday nights at 11:59 PM, Tucson time.**

	Dates	*Unit*	*Content*	*Work*
1	1/22– 1/27	**Introduction to the Online Research Lab**	**Reading:** -Welcome to the Information Fog by W. Badke **Videos:** -Information Overload -Information Overload in a Digitized World **Tutorials:** -Information Timeline -Who Wants to Be a Millionaire	Assignment 1 Discussion Quiz 1

2	1/28–2/3	**Background Information**	**Readings:** -Encyclopedia article on your topic -CQ Researcher article on your topic **Tutorials** -How to Write an MLA Citation -MLA Style Guide	Assignment 2 Discussion
3	2/4–2/10	**Media Bias**	**Readings** -Media Bias -Viewpoint 1 article -Viewpoint 2 article	Assignment 3 Discussion
4	2/11–2/17	**Popular and Scholarly Sources**	**Tutorial** -Popular and Scholarly Sources: The Game -Primary Research Article **Videos** -Scholarly Sources versus Popular Sources -What Is a Scholarly Article? **Readings** -Scholarly article on your topic -Popular article on your topic	Assignment 4 Quiz: Units 1–4
5	2/18–2/24	**Evaluating Web Resources**	**Tutorial** -Evaluating Information on the Web -Evaluating Web Resources **Video** -Wikiality	Assignment 5

| 6 | 2/25–3/3 | **Using the UA Library Catalog** | **Tutorials**
 -Searching the Library Catalog
 -Finding and Using Ebooks with Ebrary
 Readings
 -Tomorrow's Academic Libraries: Maybe Even Some Books
 -Hamlet's Blackberry: Why Paper Is Eternal | Assignment 6
 Discussion |
| 7 | 3/4–3/8 | **Searching Effectively** | **Tutorials**
 -How to Search Effectively
 -Searching Academic Search Complete
 -Finding an Article When You Have a Citation | Assignment 7 |

3/09–3/17
HAVE A GREAT SPRING BREAK!

8	3/18–3/24	**Using More Databases**	**Tutorials** -Searching JSTOR -Searching LexisNexis Academic	Assignment 8 Quiz: Units 5–8
9	3/25–3/31	**Avoiding Plagiarism**	**Tutorials** -Avoiding Plagiarism -In-text Citations **Reading** -Plagiarism and Cheating: Are They Becoming More Acceptable in the Internet Age?	Assignment 9 Discussion
10	4/1–4/7	**Review**	**Tutorial** -Comprehensive Review Tutorial on Research Basics	Assignment 10
11	4/8–4/14	Final Project & Final Exam		

Grading
Letter grades will be awarded as follows:
- A = 90–100%
- B = 80–89%
- C = 70–79%
- D = 60–69%
- F = 0–59%

Course Requirements
The ORL is worth a total of **500 points**, divided as follows:
- **Three Quizzes (25 points each, total 75 points):** Quizzes will cover material posted on D2L and must be taken individually by the student. With the exception of Quiz 1, quizzes may be taken twice. Students will receive the higher of the two quiz scores.
- **Five Discussions (15 points each, total 75 points):** Participation grades will stem from five discussions. For each discussion, students must post a thoughtful, unique answer to a question. Students should build an informed response between Monday morning (when the question is posted) and Sunday night (when your response is due). Part of your grade will be based on your interactions with your fellow students, which requires that you read and respond to other posts as well.
- **Ten Assignments (25 points each, total 250 points):** Assignments will be used to assess your understanding of content delivered via tutorials, readings, etc. To receive full points, assignments should have minimal spelling, grammar, or other mechanical errors and submitted through the D2L Dropbox before the deadline. Do *not* e-mail them to me.
- **Final Project (50 points):** The final project will consist of a short writing project and annotated bibliography based on the topic that you choose for this course.
- **Final Exam (50 points):** The comprehensive final exam will be a multiple-choice test delivered online via D2L. It will cover material from the entire semester.

Course Policies

Late Work Policies
- All work must be submitted by 11:59 PM (Tucson time) on the day it is due. After that time, the dropbox will close. To be fair to students who submit work on time, late submissions are not accepted.

- If you find that you are unable to meet a deadline due to circumstances beyond your control, please e-mail at least three (3) days in advance. I am willing to make accommodations for special cases, but I do expect students to take responsibility of their learning by planning ahead.
- Internet connectivity problems do not count as a catastrophe. Wi-Fi is available on campus and throughout Tucson. Same thing goes for computer problems. Get a flash drive so you can get your documents to another machine and uploaded, in case of emergency. D2L outages are documented on the system; if the system does go down at the exact moment of a stated deadline, you will not be penalized.
- **You are responsible for ensuring that an assignment has been successfully submitted.** Get in the habit of checking your e-mail after submitting an assignment to ensure that it went through. If you claim you submitted an assignment that I never received, you must be able to back it up with an e-mail verification (for the record, I have submitted dozens of items through dropbox for my online classes, and I've never failed to receive a verification e-mail).
- **Complete the assignments ahead of time in case you encounter problems and need to contact me or D2L.** If you are unfamiliar with D2L, please review the following web site: http://help.d2l.arizona.edu/ students/home.
- Minor illnesses, vacations, court dates, and hangovers, although perhaps inevitable, are not considered legitimate excuses for late or missed work.
- Medical and dean's excuses will be accepted. These excuses must be officially documented.

Class Conduct
All UA students are responsible for upholding the Student Code of Conduct, which can be read online at http://deanofstudents.arizona.edu/student codeofconduct.

Accessibility and Accommodations
It is the university's goal that learning experiences be as accessible as possible. If you anticipate or experience physical or academic barriers based on disability, please let me know immediately so that we can discuss options. You are also welcome to contact Disability Resources (XXX) XXX– XXXX to establish reasonable accommodations.

Student Code of Academic Integrity
Students are encouraged to share intellectual views and discuss freely the principles and applications of course materials. However, graded work/

exercises must be the product of independent effort unless otherwise instructed. Students are expected to adhere to the UA Code of Academic Integrity as described in the UA General Catalog. See http://deanofstudents .arizona.edu/codeofacademicintegrity.

Confidentiality of Student Records

http://www.registrar.arizona.edu/ferpa/default.htm

Subject to Change

Information contained in the course syllabus may be subject to change with advance notice, as deemed appropriate by the instructor.

APPENDIX 2

Resource 4.2

Sample Syllabus Graduate Information Literacy Course

LIBR 696a—Information Research Strategies for Graduate Students and Researchers Summer 2013 Syllabus

Description of Course

LIBR 696a is designed to provide a foundation for graduate level library research. The ten-week (10-week) online course addresses topics such as database searching, managing citations, literature reviews, information access policies, scholarly communication issues, and copyright basics. The course is open to graduate students and researchers in all departments and disciplines.

Instructor Information:

This course is taught by Jane Smith, Associate Librarian at the University Libraries.

> Jane Smith
> Office Location: Main Library, Rm A208
> Telephone number: XXXXX
> E-mail address: XXXXXX

Instructor working hours are generally from 9 AM to 6 PM weekdays. Contact your instructors by phone or e-mail with questions or concerns. They will respond as soon as possible, usually within twenty-four (24) hours.

Course Goals:

The course will:

- Provide graduate students and researchers with a foundation for searching, locating, and managing information for their graduate courses and research.
- Examine the legal and ethical issues of information access and use.

Course Learning Outcomes:

Students will be able to:

- Demonstrate knowledge and use of information sources in their discipline and related disciplinary areas.
- Successfully create and apply search strategies.
- Effectively manage citations using a bibliographic management program.
- Apply ethical and legal standards in their use of information.

Course Methodology

LIBR 696a will be taught online through Desire2Learn (D2L). Modules are released one week at a time on Sundays at 12:01 AM. Teaching and learning is accomplished through a combination of readings, tutorials, slide presentations, asynchronous discussions, written assignments, and a course project.

Course Project

For the LIBR 696a course project you will create an online research portfolio containing selected information tools and resources in your disciplinary area that you discover throughout the course. Details on the course project will be provided in Week 1 and instructions for setting up the research portfolio web site given in Week 2. A peer critique assignment around the portfolio is scheduled in Week 8. Your final research portfolio is due at the end of Week 9 on August 4.

Required Texts

There are no textbooks to purchase for LIBR 696a. Course readings will consist of journal articles and other full-text linked materials. Unless otherwise noted, all readings will be required and will be available on the course site.

Hardware/Software Requirements

Students must have the latest version of the Flash Player installed on their computers. For more information on operating system and browser minimum requirements for D2L, visit D2L System Requirements (http://help.d2l.arizona.edu/students/system_requirements).

Required Skills
Basic computer and internet skills are required.

Technology Assistance
  D2L Student Help pages: http://help.d2l.arizona.edu/students/home.
  D2L technology assistance: 24/7 IT Support Center http://uits.arizona.edu/
  departments/the247
  RefWorks help: RS-RWinformation@refworks-cos.com

Library Assistance
If you need immediate assistance (when instructors are not available) with library databases, the catalog and other information resources, please contact the Ask a Librarian Service (http://www.library.arizona.edu/ask), or call the Main Library Information and Reference Help desk: (520) 621–6442.

Grading Policy
Grades are based on the following:

Assignments (8)	200 pts
Discussions (3)	60 pts
Research Portfolio (4)	100 pts
Quizzes (3)	15 pts
Class Participation	25 pts
Total	**400 pts**

Letter grades for the course will be awarded as follows:

A = 90–100%
B = 80–89%
C = 70–79%
D = 60–69%
F = 0–59%

Assignment Deadlines:
All assignments, discussions, and the research portfolio must be submitted by the specified due date. Students are responsible for assuring proper delivery of their assignments/final project. D2L sometimes experiences service interruptions. Please plan to have your reading and assignments done well before the due date. Points will be deducted from earned score for late submissions: 10 percent points deducted for up to one day late; 20 percent points for 2–7

days late. Assignments submitted more than one week after the due date will have 50 percent points deducted from earned score.

If there is an exceptional reason for late submissions, please notify the instructors as soon as possible (preferably before the deadline).

Instructor Feedback

Instructor feedback on assignments will be given individually to students through the D2L Dropbox within seven (7) days after the assignment due date. Students are expected to review the instructor feedback and respond to instructor questions.

Class Participation

Class participation by students includes reading course module content as well as reviewing and responding to instructor assignment feedback and questions/comments in online discussions or e-mails. In the grading scheme, a total of twenty-five (25) points is possible for class participation.

Class Conduct

All UA students are responsible for upholding the Student Code of Conduct, which can be read online at http://deanofstudents.arizona.edu/policiesand-codes/studentcodeofconduct.

Academic Integrity

Students are encouraged to share intellectual views and discuss freely the principles and applications of course materials. However, graded work/exercises must be the product of independent effort unless otherwise instructed. Students are expected to adhere to the UA Code of Academic Integrity as described in the UA General Catalog. See: http://deanofstudents.arizona.edu/sites/deanofstudents.arizona.edu/files/code_of_academic_integrity.pdf.

Special Needs and Accommodations

Students who need special accommodation or services should contact the Disability Resources Center, 1224 East Lowell Street, Tucson, AZ 85721, (520) 621–3268, FAX (520) 621–9423, e-mail: uadrc@email.arizona.edu, http://drc.arizona.edu/.

You must register and request that the Center or DRC send official notification of your accommodation needs to your instructors as soon as possible. Please plan to meet with one or both of your instructors by appointment to discuss accommodations and how the course requirements and activities may impact your ability to fully participate. *The need for accommodations must be documented by the appropriate office.*

Confidentiality of Student Records
http://www.registrar.arizona.edu/privacyguidelines.htm

Subject to Change Statement
Information contained in the course syllabus may be subject to change, as deemed appropriate by the instructors. Students will be notified of such changes.

Course Schedule

Week	Topics	Assignments & Due Dates
Week 1 **June 3–8**	Module 1: Introduction to the Course	Module 1: Introduce yourself. (10 pts)—June 9
	Module 2: The Information Search Process	Module 2: Reflection on the Information Search Process. (25 pts)—June 9
Week 2 **June 9–16**	Module 1: Effective Search Strategies	Pre-Test. (5 pts)—June 9 Module 1: Creating search strategies. (25 pts)—June 16
	Module 2: Setting up the Research Portfolio Website	Module 2: Set up your research portfolio website. (25 pts)—June 23
Week 3 **Jun 16–23**	Citation Management	Setting up RefWorks and exporting citations. (25 pts)—June 23
Week 4 **June 23–30**	Disciplinary Databases	**Reminder:** Wk 2, Mod 2 assignment due June 23. Searching disciplinary databases and exporting citations into RefWorks. (25 pts)—June 30
Week 5 **June 30– July 7**	Multidisciplinary Databases	Searching multi-disciplinary databases and exporting citations into RefWorks. (25 pts)—July 14 [**Note** the different deadline for this assignment!]

Week 6 **July 7–14**	Introduction to the Literature Review/ Searching for Dissertations and Theses	Exploring Dissertations/Theses & Literature Reviews. (25 pts)—July 14 Mid-course evaluation. (5 pts)—July 14 **Reminder:** Wk 5 assignment due July 14.
Week 7 **July 14–21**	Scholarly Communication and Open Access	Open Access Publishing. (25 pts)—July 21 Share link to Research Portfolio website with assigned class partner. (5 points)—July 21
Week 8 **July 21–28**	Copyright and Fair Use	1. Discussion on Copyright Scenario. (25 pts) a. Post response to scenario. July 23 b. Post a question or comment to guest instructor Dan Lee, Copyright librarian. July 24 c. Post a substantive comment on another student's post. July 28 2. Research Portfolio peer review. (20 pts)—July 28
Week 9 **July 28–** **Aug 4**	Social Media and Scholarly Networking	1. Value of social media in scholarly networking. (25 pts)—Aug 4 2. Share link to final Research Portfolio with instructors. (50 pts)—Aug 4

Week 10 **Aug 4–7**	End-of-Course Reflection	End of Course Reflection. (25 pts)—Aug 7
		Post-Test. (5 pts)—Aug 7

NOTES

1. Judith Grunert O'Brien, Barbara J. Mills, and Margaret W. Cohen, *The Course Syllabus: A Learning Centered Approach*, 2nd ed. (San Francisco: John Wiley & Sons, 2008).

2. Jennifer Sinor and Matt Kaplan. "Creating Your Syllabus," University of Michigan Center for Research on Learning and Teaching, available at http://www.crlt.umich.edu/gsis/p2_1, accessed June 1, 2013.

3. Ibid.

4. Grunert O'Brien, Mills and Cohen, *The Course Syllabus*, 12.

5. Ibid., 6.

6. Sinor and Kaplan, "Creating Your Syllabus."

7. Marilla Svinicki and Wilbert J. McKeachie, *McKeachie's Teaching Tips: Strategies, Research, and Theory for College and University Teachers,* 13th ed. (Belmont, CA : Wadsworth, Cengage Learning, 2011), 17.

8. Linda B. Nilson, *The Graphic Syllabus and the Outcomes Map* (San Francisco: Jossey Bass, 2007), 1.

9. Barbara E. Walvoord and Virginia Johnson Anderson, *Effective Grading: A Tool for Learning and Assessment in College*, 2nd ed. (San Francisco: Jossey-Bass, 2010), 113.

10. John C. Ory and Katherine E. Ryan. *Tips for Improving Testing and Grading* (Newbury Park, CA: Sage Publications, 1993), 116.

11. Ibid.

12. Barbara Gross Davis, *Tools for Teaching* (San Francisco: Jossey-Bass, 1993), 289.

13. Walvoord and Anderson, *Effective Grading*, 113–114.

14. Ibid., 114–115.

15. Sinor and Kaplan, "Creating Your Syllabus"; Grunert O'Brien, Mills, and Cohen, *The Course Syllabus,* 39–110; Sharon Calhoon and Angela Becker, "How Students Use the Course Syllabus," *International Journal for the Scholarship of Teaching and Learning* 2, no. 1 (2008). http://academics.georgiasouthern.edu/ijsotl/v2n1/articles/Calhoon-Becker/Article_Calhoon-Becker.pdf.

16. Sylvie L. F. Richards, "The Interactive Syllabus: A Resource-based, Constructivist Approach to Learning," (Paper presented at EDUCAUSE 2001 Conference, Indianapolis, Indiana, October 2001), available at http://net.educause.edu/ir/library/pdf/EDU01108.pdf, accessed June 1, 2013.

17. Ibid.

18. Scott Windham, "The Interactive Syllabus: Modifications and New Insights," *Innovate: Journal of Online Education* 4, no. 6 (2008), available at http://citeseerx .ist.psu.edu/viewdoc/download?doi=10.1.1.186.5203&rep=rep1&type=pdf, accessed January 15, 2014.

19. Svinicki and McKeachie, *McKeachie's Teaching Tips*, 15.

20. Calhoon and Becker, "How Students Use the Course Syllabus."

21. Anne-Marie Armstrong, "Integrating Learning and Collaboration Using an Interactive Online Course Syllabus," (refereed paper presented at the Annual TCC Worldwide Online Conference, 2011), available at http://etec.hawaii.edu/proceedings/2011/ Armstrong.pdf, accessed January 15, 2014.

22. Ibid.

23. Calhoon and Becker, "How Students Use the Course Syllabus."

24. Ibid.

25. Ibid.

26. Ibid.

Section Two

DEVELOPING THE UNITS

Chapter Five

Learning Materials 101: Variety Is the Spice of Life

INTRODUCTION

During graduate school, Yvonne, one of the authors, took an online course that consisted of a weekly reading from the course text followed by a weekly quiz. There were also mid-term and final exams and one cumulative assignment. This was in the early days of online courses, so we can cut the instructor some slack, but the course can be easily summed up in one word: boring. The instructor did not take advantage of any of the social media or multimedia tools available at the time. There was little to no interaction with other students or with the instructor, and the entire course was passive and reading-centered. Additionally, the lack of any type of video, audio lecture, or practical assignment led to a flat, uninspired, and frustrating experience for most students. This text-heavy class may have proved interesting for the student that favored a more verbal style of learning, but students with other learning preferences most likely found the course difficult to get through.

Like a face-to-face course, an online course can and should include a variety of materials from hands-on practice to instructional videos to multimedia lectures and group projects. In this chapter, we take a look at the array of materials that you can use in your online IL courses. We also offer tips and best practices for different types of tools and media for delivering content and maximizing learning through engagement.

UNDERLYING TEACHING STRATEGIES

A basic drawback of the one-shot library session is that too often librarians only have enough time to simply *present* information to students rather than to create and deliver a lesson or multiple lessons that allow for the acquisition of new concepts and skills. The ACRL Information Literacy Standards represent lifelong learning competencies that lend themselves to a constructivist teaching approach. Constructivist learning theory states that learning occurs when students build on prior knowledge to create new meaning; students are active participants in their own learning, create new knowledge and understanding through interacting with others, and gain deep learning through real-life, authentic activities.[1] Thus, one library session, one screencast, or one tutorial is not sufficient to truly learn a new skill or concept. To acquire new knowledge and skills, students should be asked to complete a number of activities in a scaffolded manner while interacting with different types of learning materials.

Here is an example of a constructivist approach for teaching literature reviews that is based on a unit in our graduate course:

> To gain a conceptual understanding, students are directed to several library web sites where they learn about the purpose of a literature review; different types of literature reviews, such as one done for a research article and one done for a review article; and the process of writing a literature review. Building on this knowledge, students are directed to locate a dissertation in their discipline and then asked to compare the dissertation literature review to what they have learned about elements of a literature review. Finally, they are asked to participate in an online discussion to share with other students their experience in reviewing the dissertation literature review and whether or not it would be the approach they would use in their own dissertation. They are also asked to comment and pose questions to other students.

This example demonstrates many constructivist principles. Students are active in their own learning while the instructor acts as a guide through the learning process. Through readings, students build on their prior knowledge of literature reviews. Students are given an authentic assignment to find a dissertation in their research area and to examine how the literature review was written. Learning is enhanced through the online discussion where students learn the diverse ways that literature reviews are presented in different disciplines and also learn from others what they might do differently. What should be noted is that this is a modified constructivist approach in that students are guided in a very structured way throughout the learning activity and in the use of the learning materials. Time constraints and the nature of the content often come into consideration when designing learning opportunities.

Here is an example from our undergraduate course unit on effective searching that follows the same principles:

> Through the discussion board students are first asked to think about how they search the web and what strategies they use. Students are then introduced to

Boolean searching through a tutorial that includes definitions, examples, and interactive activities. Students then complete a Guide on the Side tutorial where they supply different search strings in Academic Search Complete and see the results from the different search strings. Students are then asked to complete a short quiz. At the end of this unit, students complete an assignment where they are asked to create their own search strings in Academic Search Complete and evaluate and adapt them as needed.

ALIGNING LEARNING MATERIALS
WITH LEARNING OUTCOMES

Q: For the following unit learning objective: "Students will be able to compare Kuhlthau's Information Search Process (ISP) model[2] to their own search process." Which of the following learning materials or activities contribute to this learning outcome?

A: Select all that apply:

a) A video showing a librarian demonstrating mind mapping to select a research topic.
b) A tutorial on Boolean logic.
c) A discussion activity where students explain their own information-seeking process and relate it to Kuhlthau's model and comment on other students' entries.
d) Reading information about the ISP model on Carol Kuhlthau's web site.

If you selected the last two options, you are on the right track. Quality Matters (QM) rubrics specify that all learning components of a course should be in alignment with both course goals and unit-level learning objectives. All learning materials and activities must promote the achievement of the unit learning objectives.[3] Certainly, students should learn about mind mapping and Boolean logic, and these learning materials would align with specific learning objectives addressing use of Boolean logic and narrowing a topic. However, the last two learning activities directly address the unit learning objective given previously.

We should not stop with these particular options just because they are consistent with the learning objective. We must also consider which materials will engage students more and which materials will be accessible to students. Should we use or create an interactive tutorial about Kuhlthau's Information Search Process to enhance student learning? What about a podcast outlining the ISP model? Would the tutorial and the podcast be accessible to everyone in the class? What about the hearing impaired? What about students that use only Mac devices where Flash does not work? What if a student does not have access to speakers on their computer? You may be thinking that this sounds like a lot of trouble and you will just assign the web page and give students a multiple-choice quiz. Students will more than likely be successful in completing the quiz, but will they be able to apply the model to their own research experience and become more self-aware and reflective learners?

When selecting learning materials, another important consideration is to match the learning approach with the content.[4] The ACRL Information Literacy Standards cover a wide range of competencies that we teach using a variety of learning approaches or strategies. For example, in teaching students how information policies affect the everyday lives of students, we could use the approach of having students read a popular magazine article about how the entertainment industry has targeted college students who illegally download music and the background history of why this is a concern for making information accessible on the Internet. To reinforce the learning, we could ask students to participate in a discussion with other students about aspects that relate to their own life experiences as a result of this information policy. Another IL concept, such as identifying appropriate library databases, would be better learned by having students complete a tutorial that provides guided practice in selecting and searching licensed databases. This is a much better approach than using a reading or simply watching a video. It is important to take the time to consider and select the teaching strategy that will work best for a specific learning outcome.

ADDRESSING LEARNING STYLES

Learning styles can be defined as a preference or ease in learning through a particular method, such as visual, auditory, or kinesthetic.[5] Although there are myriads of learning style theories, there is no evidence that any of these theories are valid or show that learning styles can be used effectively to match with types of learning materials or activities.[6] In fact there is more evidence to support the idea that *all* learners benefit from multiple types of activities and materials designed for specific learning styles when attempting to understand new complex concepts.[7] This does not mean that learners do not have preferences in how they want to learn new concepts, and it is our responsibility as course designers to ensure that a variety of learning materials and activities are used throughout the course to accommodate different learning preferences. In addition, using a variety of learning materials and approaches prevents the course from becoming boring through rote learning and the presentation of the same type of material for each module.[8]

An example of using a variety of types of learning materials and activities is a unit on copyright and fair use in our online graduate course. We first have students view an interactive, multimedia tutorial "Fair Use and Copyright in Instruction" developed in-house. They are then directed to the Copyright Genie[9] to determine if a book written in 1979 and finally published in 1999 is under copyright protection. For their weekly assignment, students are given a scenario about viewing selections of a Hollywood movie and an entire documentary in a course. In an online discussion, they are asked to discuss the fair use aspects of using these materials. Students must respond to questions and comments with the invited guest, the Library's Director of the Office of Copyright Management & Scholarly Communication at least twice and once with another student concerning fair use issues. From this example, the learning materials and activities require students to read, carry out an action, reflect, write, and engage with others on the concepts of copyright and fair use. The discussion conversations make it clear that students have developed a deeper understanding of the Fair Use guidelines and how they can be applied to their own teaching activities.

CREATING THE MATERIALS

What follows are best practices that we have found for using a variety of types of learning materials and activities with examples from our own courses on teaching specific IL concepts.

Discussions

Just about every book or article on online learning that you will encounter will tell you that discussions are a must for a successful course because of the myriad of benefits they offer: community building, a place for students to learn from and interact with one another, and a place for students to write more freely and brainstorm ideas. However, we have found that most students dread them.

When we created our first online undergraduate course we included weekly discussions where students posted reactions to some of the content they looked at that week. Here are some of these early discussion questions:

- Discuss your search strategy and how it changed. Respond to other students' posts and offer suggestions on how they can improve their own search.
- Discuss which database you liked best and why. Respond to other students' posts.

These types of discussion questions led to indifferent, flat, and short, at most one to two lines, posts. Responses to other students were even worse and rarely went beyond the "I agree" stage.

To improve our student discussions, we began to create discussions that included both intrinsic and extrinsic motivators for students. Rovai describes intrinsic motivation as one that is inspired by "personal interest and enjoyment" and extrinsic motivation as "motivation induced by external factors,"[10] such as peer evaluations or grades. We wanted students to enjoy posting, to feel passionate about a topic and want to share their opinions and ideas with other students, and we wanted to create a forum where students looked forward to reading other students' posts and learning from one another. Our goal then was to create "a learning environment that motivates students to engage in positive social interaction and active engagement in learning."[11] We accomplished this by asking students to respond to more provocative controversial course topics and readings. Here are two examples we found successful with students. These questions have generated much longer, more in-depth, inspired, and energetic student posts:

- Similar to the college in Boston that you read about this week, our university library will most likely remove all of the print material including books next year. Do you think this is a good idea? Why or why not?
- This week you read two articles with opposing viewpoints on your topic. In your opinion which author did a better job of supporting their argument? Use excerpts from the articles to back up your opinion.

Even though these questions were more interesting to students and generated significantly better posts, we still needed external motivators to ensure students would post as required. These external motivators include points for original posts and for responses to others, a word or sentence minimum, an overall participation grade based on number of authored and read discussions, and a deadline. Below are some other best practices for discussions:

- Be prescriptive: Your discussion prompt should tell students exactly what you wish from them. If you want them to cite from an article, you need tell them how many examples they should include. Similarly, if you would like discussions to include both a reflection and a summary, you must specify this in your prompt.
- Include a minimum number of posts and responses: Students are often pressed for time and many will only post minimally. Let students know the number of posts they should have each week and how many responses to other students' posts they should make. Using an exact number or a minimum number is best.

- Have deadlines for original posts and responses: To have more robust discussions, students need to post throughout the week and respond to one another. However, most students will wait until the end of the week, usually hours before a module closes to complete tasks. To avoid this, we have found it useful to have a mid-week due date for a first post and an end-of-the-week due date for a response to a post.
- Base posts on topics that lend themselves to discussion and not on personal reflections to homework or tools: As mentioned, responses to questions based on issues, preferably more provocative, controversial issues, and for which students have some background knowledge work best. We have found that scenario questions where students are asked to solve a problem also work well. You should avoid questions where students will have the same or similar answers, such as their reaction to a new database.
- Give students a few discussion options to choose from: Not all topics will appeal to all students, so most of our discussion prompts include at least two questions that students can choose from.
- Allow students to rate each others' posts: Many LMSs include a ratings option where students can rate posts with stars. Students can be told that posts with the highest ratings will receive extra-credit points.
- Be involved in posts and respond to them yourself: There is nothing more motivating to a discussion than having the instructor being an integral part of it. Students may not respond to your posts directly, but they want to know that the instructor is part of the conversation and is reading what they have to say. Thus, you should be an active member of all discussions even though you will not have the time to respond to all posts. In larger online courses, you can select a few posts to respond to each week.
- Provide clear rubrics so students can see what and how they will be graded: Students should be told ahead of time how many posts will be evaluated and graded. Discussions can be graded individually and assessed for content and length, or they can be graded in the aggregate as overall participation points. We have found that the former is incredibly time consuming and does not lead to higher quality or more frequent posts.
- Have closing dates: Online discussions are akin to weekly in-class meetings and they can help to keep students on track. Discussions should have opening and closing dates to ensure that students are not waiting until the last few weeks of the course to start posting.

Readings

Articles and books are often the backbone of any course, and the online environment is no different. Readings provide more in-depth information than what can be presented in a typical LMS format or in a lecture while adding another perspective. However, like other course materials, when selecting readings you should make sure that they play an integral part of the course and that they are truly needed for students to complete a unit. Many IL courses are much more skills-based than other types of courses and may not lend themselves to course readings. If you feel that a reading would be a really good idea, but students will not need it to fully participate in other unit activities, offer it is a suggested reading instead. Also, keep in mind that today's student is accustomed to just skimming and scanning digital text. For a longer reading, you can ask students to only read selected sections. It is also important to choose authoritative, objective readings from respected sources. All readings should include a citation to model expectations for trustworthy sources and how they should be cited.

In our undergraduate course, we made a radical change when we noticed that students were still having difficulties using quality information sources in their final cumulative assignment. After analyzing student work we realized that students were struggling to locate adequate resources because they were still having difficulties understanding their topic and thus, could not research it well. This led us to change the first few weeks of the course from a searching tools emphasis to a critical reading one where students first got to know their topic through course readings preselected for them. Students have reacted overwhelmingly positive to these readings, and their final assignments have improved greatly. Through these preselected readings, students become literate in their chosen topic and learn about the different types of information resources available today from blog entries and wiki articles to scholarly sources.

There are certain information literacy topics, such as scholarly communication, open access to information, and copyright law that lend themselves to readings that can provide different perspectives and more in-depth information. For these types of topics in our graduate course, we use readings for students to delve deeper into a topic. We use web resources from trusted academic libraries and educational institutions and digital higher education news sources, such as *The Chronicle of Higher Education* and *Inside Higher Ed*. We have found reading sources from library listservs, Twitter postings, Google searches, research articles, and other IL online courses. When linking to readings we include a descriptive label to let students know what they are linking to. For some topics we provide supplemental readings for those graduate students who want to learn more on their own.

Lectures

Delivering content through a lecture format seems like a wasted opportunity in an online environment where there are other teaching strategies that use the latest education technology for increased interactivity and engagement. But let us start with the benefits and advantages. Having students view a lecture is a way for them to be introduced to the content without doing a lot of reading. This can help engage students who are easily bored with readings and who need different types of stimulation. However, a lecture may not lead to the same type of retention that a reading can offer. Fortunately, in the online environment lectures captured digitally can be played back at the student's convenience and repeated as needed for note taking or for an exam review. Additionally, providing a table of contents and transcribing the lecture will make it much more usable for students who want to dip in and out of lecture topics of interest or importance to them, or those students needing more time to engage with the material.

The current state of lecture capture software makes it relatively easy to record a lecture with audio, video, and presentation slides. The digital recording can be stored and integrated into the LMS course site for students to review at their convenience. Examples of commercial products used in higher education include Panopto, Mediasite from Sonic Foundry, Articulate, and Captivate. In an online course, using lecture capture software can be beneficial for providing a more personal approach to delivering content.

Best practices for using lecture capture software include the following guidelines.[12] These practices also apply to creating a podcast or a screencast.

- Prepare for your recording by setting aside enough time to learn how to use the software.
- Get technical support for setting up the software, which may require downloading client software and hardware, such as a microphone and a webcam.
- Use a good quality microphone and record in a quiet room with little ambient noise.
- Test the audio and video quality. Students may give up on a poor quality recording.
- Practice recording and uploading the lecture so that you are not distracted by the technology during the recording.
- If you are using copyrighted materials, limit the access to students within the LMS course site.
- Ensure that your students have the necessary software and hardware to view the materials.
- Keep the lecture to no more than thirty minutes.[13]

Podcasts

There are low-tech, low-costs ways to record and distribute audio, video, and computer screens in the form of podcasts and screencasts. Podcasts serve the same purpose as readings or lectures and may be a preferred form of learning for students with busy course and work schedules because they can be played on mobile devices. Podcasts provide students control over their own learning in their own time frame and location and can add elements of "novelty and engagement."[14] Podcasts also work better for students with reading difficulties. Many students may be familiar with podcasts for entertainment purposes and will welcome a technology that they already use.

Podcasts can be created for free using software programs, such as Audacity, Podomatic, or podcasting tools available through your LMS. Podcasts require time for planning and editing, just as you would for designing a lecture or a tutorial, although it will not take as much time as creating a video lecture and could provide the same value. Kidd outlines key points for creating an effective audio podcast:[15]

- Make the podcast short (three to eight minutes) to keep students interested.
- Introduce the topic at the beginning with an outline of what will be covered.
- Number and summarize points throughout the Podcast, so students can locate where they are in the podcast.
- Summarize the content at the end of the Podcast using the same keywords used in the beginning.

For clear and simple instructions on how to create a podcast, see Melissa Purcell's article, "The Power of Podcasting."[16]

Screencasts

A screencast is a digital recording of the activity taking place on a computer screen with accompanying audio commentary.[17] Screencasts are useful for showing rather than telling students a set of instructions, such as demonstrating how to create an account in RefWorks and organize citations into folders.[18] Screencasts showing students how to use a database have become prevalent in libraries, but they are beginning to lose their popularity partially as a result of their lack of any interactivity. We use screencasts sparingly and only when another type of activity (interactive tutorial or reading) will not work well. When using screencasts, they should be kept short because longer screencasts can be frustrating for students to have to listen or view the material in a linear fashion to find the information they need.[19] Screencasts work best when are used to present small chunks of information followed by an activity where students can practice what they have learned and receive feedback. Although screencasts are relatively easy to create, editing them, especially when there is an audio component, can be time consuming.

Video

Nothing can break up the monotony of class that is centered on readings and lectures than a video. Even though watching videos is a passive form of instruction, they can be attention-grabbing and stimulating for students, and with sites like YouTube and Vimeo, it has never been easier to use videos in the online classroom. In addition, using video can be incredibly time saving for instructors. There are already numerous quality videos from libraries on a wide range of information literacy topics that can be easily searched on the web and embedded into your course. Videos should be used to extend content beyond what you provide through your own lectures, readings, and tutorials; use them to clarify a concept, for demonstration, or to introduce a topic. You do not want to use a video if your learning objective is to teach students how to use a database. Remember, videos are passive and do not allow for any type of interaction or application of skills. Lastly, to maximize their benefits, videos should be short in length, under five minutes.

Web Conferencing

Many LMSs now have a web conferencing tool with features such as desktop sharing, ability to annotate whiteboards, presentations and other content, and a survey tool to get immediate feedback from students. Web conferencing can be used like a lecture or readings to present course content. It can be used to engage students by having them ask questions and get immediate feedback. Web conferencing can also be used to bring in guest speakers and hold student discussions.[20] In our graduate course, we used web conferences to hold online office hours. Although this was a voluntary activity, several students showed up to ask questions about use of the citation management software and the final project. While this activity could have been carried out through an asynchronous discussion forum, it was a worthwhile to provide an opportunity to interact more personally in real-time with students.

The downside of using web conferencing is scheduling a time where students from various time zones can participate. In addition, web conferencing requires a great deal of bandwidth and a high-speed Internet connection for maximum effectiveness.[21] Although the current state of web conferencing has greatly improved, audio or screen sharing problems are common. During a live session, this is a frustrating and time wasting experience for both instructors and students. Synchronous learning tools such as web conferences should be used sparingly in online courses because one of the advantages of online learning is that students have the flexibility to interact and reflect on the learning materials in their own time frame, which can lead to more thoughtful responses to assignments.[22]

Setting up the web conference program and feeling comfortable using the technology takes practice. Before a web conference, provide students with clear instructions on how to access the web conference program, what will be presented, and what they will need to prepare ahead of time. Recommend that they run a test on their computer for audio/video functionality before the scheduled time. You should also include information on how to get technical support. At the beginning of the web conference, orient students to the web conferencing functions that will be used and record the session, so that students who are absent can view the event later. In our experience, a webcam is not necessary, and it can distract from the main presentation. In addition, encourage students to use a microphone instead of overusing chat, which can lead to long, disjointed messages and slow down the discussion.

Games

A good game like those that students are accustomed to includes characters, adaptive interaction, amazing graphics, multiple audio elements, and an engaging storyline that keeps them coming back for more. It is most unlikely that you will have the resources to develop a great or even a really good game that includes characters, graphics, a storyline with multiple variables, and outcomes. However, you can include elements that make games so attractive to students. These include the accumulation of points, levels students can move through, leader boards that display how students are doing, and scenario-based learning where students must find a solution to a problem.[23]

Games such as puzzles, small group competitions and scavenger hunts can be used for an orientation to the syllabus or the library web site. Game-like tutorials add playful elements, such as role playing, offering choices in topics to review, and matching definitions and descriptions. In our undergraduate course, we created a "Who Wants to Be a Millionaire" game where students are asked about different course policies that they should have read about in the syllabus. Students are rewarded with an increase in money and a move to another level until they reach the end and "win" the big jackpot.

Digital badges can be used to motivate students to access and learn online course content by awarding badges for different skill areas after students have completed a number of tasks. Part of the motivation comes from students being able to visually display what they have learned or accomplished. They are similar to the physical badges Girl Scouts receive after completing certain tasks. Students can display their digital badges on social media sites to show the skills they have mastered. Current leaders in digital badge programs are Purdue University (Passport),[24] the Mozilla Foundation (Open Badges),[25] and HASTAC (Badges for Lifelong Learning).[26]

Using the badge approach is similar to creating a course unit in that it includes learning objectives, a variety of materials, and assessments resulting in a badge. We are currently using badges in our undergraduate course to better track student work. After students complete a tutorial or a reading, they must correctly answer a series of questions to complete a task. After completing several tasks they are granted a digital badge and can then begin work on another badge. Students receive either individualized feedback from the instructor for long answers, or automated feedback as part of a multiple choice question. Digital badges are in their infancy, and it is still not known how well higher education institutions and employers will accept them as a representation of a student's skills and knowledge. However, they do present one more tool in an instructor's toolkit of student motivators.

Social Media

From YouTube videos to Pinterest boards to WordPress blogs, the web is awash in social media tools that can be successfully used in the online course. Social media tools allow the instructor to create environments in which students and instructors can come together to share knowledge, comment on each other's work, and build community. Although the LMS can serve many of these functions, they are more limited in what they can do and what students and instructors can share. The LMS is often limited to the sharing of discussion posts and entries in a class blog. They are also less user friendly and much less visually appealing. Even though LMSs are adding more and more functionality with each upgrade, most still lag behind social media tools.

Using external social media tools has many benefits including building a greater sense of community and producing work that is more dynamic and collaborative. Because most students will already have a presence in social media networks and are already familiar with using them, they will be able to share more than just a quick introductory biographical post. They can share pictures, videos, interests, and information on events that they are attending; all of which can help to personalize the class and students to feel less isolated in the often impersonal online course. Having students post work as part of a class blog or wiki can lead to greater motivation and higher quality work because students can see one another's work and contribute to and comment on it. This idea of an authentic audience (an audience other than the instructor) can be taken further if the audience includes those outside the classroom and even outside the learning institute. Michele Van Hoeck, a librarian at California State University, Maritime, had her students research a topic and then post an article on Wikipedia.[27] She found that students were more motivated to complete their work than they had been in previous semesters.

There is a multitude of social networking tools already being used in education and with every passing year the number seems to expand greatly. Additionally, as with most web-based tools and social networks, what is popular today will be gone tomorrow. We have included a list of the more well-known social media tools that are being used in education:

- Twitter
- Facebook
- Google +
- WordPress
- Wikipedia
- WikiSpaces
- YouTube
- Vimeo
- Padlet
- Learnist
- Wordle
- Voicethread

For the many benefits that using external social media tools have, they have yet to be widely adapted by instructors. A 2012 higher education survey by Pearson Learning Solutions found that only 20 percent of respondents regularly used social media tools (blogs and wikis) in the classroom.[28] The most common reasons for not using these tools concerned academic integrity, privacy issues, and concerns over students having to set-up and use multiple accounts. In her analysis of the survey, Tinti-Kane offers a number of strategies to overcome these barriers to adoption including creating a single, closed classroom account on a site like Twitter, limiting what is used on these sites, or only using the social media functionalities that are available within the LMS. As pointed out previously, with LMSs adding more sophisticated social media functionalities, this latter option may be the best way to control privacy issues.

LMS Course Home Page

Although not part of the unit content, the course home page and assignment guide, or course shell, are two essential parts of the course you will need to create. The course home page is the first element of your course that students will encounter. As such it needs to both grab student's attention and allow students to easily figure out where they need to go. Unfortunately many LMSs default to a bland and often confusing welcome page. Figure 5.1 shows our LMS's default course home page. This welcome page is too text heavy,

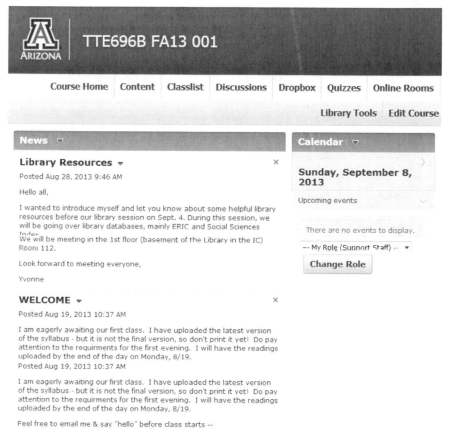

Figure 5.1. Default Course Home Page

does not grab the student's attention in any way, nor does it make it clear that the student must click on the "Content" tab if they wish to start the course.

To make the course home page more intuitive, we created a custom page using an HTML editor and then imported it into the LMS (Fig. 5.2). In contrast, this page is more visually stimulating and easier to navigate; students know exactly where they need to go to get started. Once students access this page, they are taken to the first page of content and from there they can easily access the additional content through arrow icons.

Because of the visual complexity of the course site, it is important to make your site as intuitive and easy to navigate as possible. Here are some other useful guidelines:

• Provide a Start Here or Read Me First module that is prominently displayed in the course site. This module can include the syllabus and course sched-

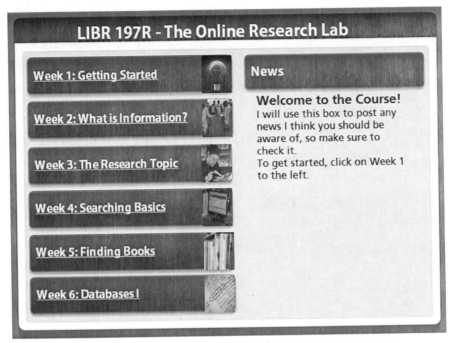

Figure 5.2. Custom Home Page with Clear Navigation

ule, advice on netiquette, orientation to the LMS, and a short questionnaire about readiness for taking an online course.

- Position the Start Here module at the top left or center of the course site. Jakob Nielsen, the well-known usability expert, was the first to establish that web users scan a web page in an F pattern.[29] First, web users scan from left to right horizontally at the top of the page. Next they scan vertically on the left and then again horizontally across the page. Finally users scan down the far left of the page.
- Link the Start Here module in multiple places in the course site. These could be within (1) the first announcement post or welcome e-mail message; (2) the course content list; and (3) the course schedule.
- Use clear and concise labels. Better to use vocabulary that is understandable to all, such as Required Readings rather than a label that is part of your jargon, and would not necessarily be understood students, such as Learning Resources.
- Use navigation wisely: It should be easy for students to move from one element of the course to another. The LMS should provide a horizontal navigation bar to move from one element to another, such as from Content to Discussions. These elements should also appear in a drop-down menu

or be displayed in a vertical menu on the left-hand side. Within a content module, there should be navigation elements, such as arrows, or words like *next* and *back* to help the user move forward and backward through the content and back to the course site.

The Assignment Guide

Also referred to as an interactive syllabus (see chapter 4), the assignment guide provides an alternative to how units or modules and their content is presented to students. The default for most LMSs is to present units as a table of contents on the course home page. We find this presentation of information stale and confusing to move through with any sense of continuity. As an alternative we suggest the creation of unit slides that can be linked from the course home page. These slides can be easily created using any HTML editor and uploaded to the LMS. For all of our courses we use Softchalk, an e-learning content authoring software that is easy to use and allows for linking to the slides as opposed to uploading them into the LMS. Any edits can be easily made in the Softchalk's cloud platform without needing to upload any files. Figure 5.3 shows a slide from our undergraduate course that was created using Softchalk. In addition to providing links to course materials, these types of slides also allow us to include lists of unit objectives and tasks, commentary on readings and other materials, and guidelines for completing assignments.

LIBR 197R
The Online Research Lab

| Contents ▼ | Next ► | Page 1 of 2   print all

Week 6: Use Information Ethically

In today's world of incredibly simple access to information, it can be quite easy to plagiarize something or violate copyright rules when you never meant to. In this unit, we will learn more about how you can avoid plagiarizing and using works that are copyrighted incorrectly. This week, you will also be introduced to a new database, JSTOR. Specifically, by the end of this week you should be able to:

- Define plagiarism, copyright, and remixing
- Evaluate scenarios for possible plagiarism
- Evaluate scenarios for copyright violations
- Describe strategies for avoiding plagiarism
- Describe JSTOR
- Use JSTOR to locate articles

CUT & PASTE

Figure 5.3. Course Content Page with Unit Outcomes and Other Links

UNIVERSAL DESIGN FOR LEARNING

The Universal Design for Learning (UDL) model incorporates good teaching practices into the design of learning materials and environments that promote learning for all students. Three guiding principles of UDL call for multiple options for how information is presented (representation); how students demonstrate their learning (action and expression) and how students engage with the learning materials (engagement).[30] An example of UDL is providing multiple formats for presenting content, such as readings, videos, and tutorials.[31] Other examples include providing a transcript of a podcast or creating online learning groups the first day of class to encourage peer support and engagement.

Current content creation software, such as rapid e-learning, web, and productivity software make it much easier to create accessible content with functionality for adding alternative text (alt text) for images, and captioning for audio/video presentations. Your LMS will most likely follow national and international standards for accessibility. If you are uncertain, look for a link to a statement about accessibility on your LMS web site. If you are using supplemental web sites or software, you will need to check for compliance with accessibility standards.[32]

Given the diversity of learners you will find in your course, there are quite a few elements in online course design that must be taken into consideration to make the course learning environment as accessible as possible. Here are some of the most common things that you can do to ensure that your content can be read by assistive technology, such as screen readers:

- Use built-in style formats in Microsoft Office products, such as Word, Excel, and PowerPoint. This means using style headings and title headings to indicate the structure of a page, such as a title or section header.
- Accessible PDF documents are searchable and have the ability to copy and paste text from the PDF document. Photocopied and scanned PDFs cannot be read by a screen reader.
- Create text versions or captions for audio and visual materials, including logos.
- Use high contrast colors in web pages so that the foreground and the background can be easily distinguished. Use the same practice for font colors. Black font on white is the best. Use simple and clearly understandable backgrounds in web sites and for fonts, use Verdana or Georgia for easy reading.[33]
- To detect and fix accessibility issues, Microsoft Office and Adobe Acrobat Professional have built-in accessibility checkers.[34] For web acces-

sibility evaluation, there is WAVE, a web accessibility evaluation tool from WebAim.[35]
- Work with staff from your campus disability services office. They can check your learning materials on their screen readers and other assistive technologies to ensure that your materials will be accessible to all of your students.[36]

USING COPYRIGHTED MATERIALS

For a tutorial you are creating about the differences in primary and secondary sources, you use a thumbnail image of a 1960s' Grateful Dead poster that you found on Wikipedia, as well as a scanned image of the headline and first paragraph of *San Francisco Chronicle* article that you copied from an online newspaper database describing the violence at the 1969 Altamont free concert and the cover page of a book published in 1971, *Rock Music in the Sixties*. You work at a nonprofit educational institution and intend to use the tutorial in your online course and make it accessible to the public on your library's web site. Do you need to get permission to legally use these copyrighted images?

Under the U.S. Copyright Law there are exceptions that allow use of copyrighted works without having to ask permission. One of those exemptions is the Fair Use Doctrine of the Copyright Law (17 USC § 107).[37] The Fair Use Doctrine gives users the right to use parts of a work for commentary, criticism, news reporting, education, scholarship, and research without having to request permission. To determine if you are on the side of fair use, you need to consider the following four factors:

1. The purpose of the use
2. The nature of the work
3. The amount and substantiality
4. The effect your use has on the market for the work.

Let's take a closer look at the four factors using our example.

1. The purpose of the use: The tutorial is intended for educational purposes in a nonprofit educational setting and will not be used for commercial purposes. These images are useful as examples of primary and secondary sources. This factor would favor fair use.
2. The nature of the work: Creative works, such as concert posters, enjoy more copyright protection than factual-based works, such as an encyclopedic entry, at least from copyright cases that have been litigated to date.[38]

Given the nature of the work, this would not be considered a fair-use case. The book cover, depending on the degree of creativity in the artwork might also disfavor fair use. The scanned newspaper article would be considered more factual in nature and might indicate fair use. So in this case, we might want to consider each image separately and try to find another image that would represent the 1960s' rock music culture that is not under copyright protection, which could be difficult.

3. The amount and substantiality of the use: It is necessary to display the entire poster as an example of 1960s' rock culture to help students learn the difference between primary and secondary sources. This works against fair use, but it is not determinative. All four factors need to be considered together. Also, you are using a thumbnail image of the poster, which is not considered a substitute for the original display of the work.[39] For the newspaper story, you use only the headline and the first paragraph of the story, so is it not a significant amount of the total newspaper article, but it may be a *substantial* part of the article, if many of the details of the event are disclosed in the amount used. You make a determination that there are many details and quotes that appear later in the article, so you decide that you are not using a substantial part of the article. In the case of the book cover, it is only a small part of the book, so this would favor fair use.

4. The effect on the potential market for the work in using the images is probably minimal. However, would it be possible for one of your students to copy the poster image and use it as an image on a t-shirt that he sells on the Internet? The size and resolution of the poster thumbnail would make the image almost impossible to reuse. An alternative would be to find a poster in the public domain,[40] or that has a Creative Commons license that allows for use if the source is cited. A Creative Commons license works with the Copyright Law to allow owners to give copyright permission to the public in the form of a legal license to share and use the work within certain parameters. For example, a Creative Commons license with the designation of CC BY-NC-SA is known as Attribution-Non-Commercial-Share Alike, which means that the copyright owner grants others the right to remix or modify the creative work for noncommerical purposes with the stipulation that the user will provide attribution and that the user will provide the same Creative Commons license to others for their creative work.[41]

Considering all of these factors together, the use of these images in the tutorial would be considered a fair use. Given the complexity of Copyright Law and how it has been interpreted in the courts, it is a good idea to consult with copyright experts on campus. The ALA Office for Intellectual Technology Policy offers a number of copyright tools to aid in determination of use of copyrighted materials, including a Fair Use Evaluator tool that guides users through the Fair Use Four Factors.[42] However, every use must be seen in context of the use and never be reduced to a simple checklist.[43]

Although no checklist will suffice in determining use of copyrighted materials, here is a short list of good practices:

- Assume everything you use is under copyright protection. There are notable exceptions, such as materials in the public domain, like works created by U.S. federal agencies.
- For digital content used in distance education, look to the TEACH Act qualifications. If it is not covered, then check the Fair Use four factors.
- Limit access to the material to those enrolled in your class.
- Use only what you need to make a point. If you do not need the whole video, do not use the whole video.
- Linking to another web site or a YouTube video is better than copying the material and embedding it on your course site.
- Giving attribution to an image or a video does not mean that you do not have to determine if your use of the work is in compliance with the Copyright Law.

KNOW THIS . . .

- Select learning materials that are directly applicable to the unit and that will contribute to the overall unit outcomes.
- To better engage students, course modules should consist of a variety of learning materials.
- Spend time matching the IL topic to the best material and activity to maximize learning; not all topics lend themselves to readings.
- Successful discussions require both intrinsic and extrinsic student motivators.
- Use UDL principles to ensure that all of your students can access the learning materials.
- Use videos that are short in duration so as not to bore students.
- Use HTML editors or e-learning content authoring tools to present content to students in a more dynamic manner.
- Lecture capture software runs the spectrum of technological sophistication. A low-cost, low-tech solution, such as a podcast or screencast may work just as well.
- Assume everything you use is under copyright protection.
- There are exceptions in the Copyright Law to having to ask for permission for use of copyrighted materials, such as the TEACH Act and the Fair Use Doctrine.

NOTES

1. Maryellen Allen, "Promoting Critical Thinking Skills in Online Information Literacy Instruction using a Constructivist Approach." *College & Undergraduate Libraries* 15, no. 1–2 (2008): 31.

2. Carol Kuhlthau, "Information Search Process," available at http://comminfo .rutgers.edu/~kuhlthau/information_search_process.htm, accessed January 15, 2014.

3. Quality Matters Program, "Higher Ed Program—Rubrics," available at https://www.qualitymatters.org/rubric, accessed January 15, 2014.

4. Julie Dirkson, *Design for How People Learn* (Berkeley, CA: New Riders, 2012).

5. Donna Dunning, "Learning Styles," in *Encyclopedia of Educational Psychology*, ed. Neil J. Salkind (Thousand Oaks, CA: SAGE Publications, Inc., 2008), 598–604.

6. Dirkson, *Design for How People Learn.*

7. Ruth Colvin Clark, *Evidence-based Training Methods: A Guide for Training Professionals* (Alexandria, VA: American Society for Training and Development, 2010).

8. Dirkson, *Design for How People Learn.*

9. American Library Association, *Copyright Tools*, available at http://www.ala .org/advocacy/copyright-tools, accessed January 15, 2014.

10. Alfred P. Rovai, "Facilitating Online Discussions Effectively," *The Internet and Higher Education* 10, no. 1 (2007): 77–88.

11. Rovai, "Facilitating Online Discussions Effectively."

12. Erping Zhu and Inger Bergom, "Lecture Capture: A Guide for Effective Use," *CRLT Occasional Paper*, no. 27 (2007), available at http://www.crlt.umich.edu/sites/default/files/resource_files/CRLT_no27.pdf, accessed January 15, 2014.

13. Patricia Desrosiers, "Integrating Video Lecture Tools in Online and Hybrid Classrooms," in *Enhancing Instruction with Visual Media: Utilizing Video and Lecture Capture*, eds. Ellen G. Smyth and John X. Voker (Hershey, PA: Information Science Reference, 2013), 27–42.

14. Warren Kidd, "Utilizing Podcasts for Learning and Teaching: A Review and Ways Forward for e-Learning Cultures," *Management in Education* 26, no. 2 (2012): 52.

15. Kidd, "Utilizing Podcasts," 55.

16. Melissa Purcell, "The Power of Podcasting," *Library Media Connection*, (Mar–April 2011): 48–49.

17. Tershia Pinder-Grover, Katie R. Green, and Joanna Mirecki Millunchick, "The Efficacy of Screencasts to Address the Diverse Academic Needs of Students in a Large Lecture Course," *Advances in Engineering Education* 2, no. 3 (2011): 1–28.

18. Educause Learning Initiative, "7 Things You Should Know About . . . Screencasting," (2006), available at http://net.educause.edu/ir/library/pdf/ELI7012.pdf, accessed January 15, 2014.

19. Educause, "7 Things."

20. Celeste Fenton and Brenda Ward Watkins, *Fluency in Distance Learning* (Charlotte, NC: Information Age Publishing, Inc., 2010), 32.

21. Zhu and Bergom, "Lecture Capture."

22. Rena M. Palloff and Keith Pratt, *Lessons from the Cyberspace Classroom: The Realities of Online Teaching* (San Francisco: Jossey-Bass, 2001), 25.

23. Larry Johnson, Samantha Adams, Malcolm Cummins, Victoria Estrada, Alex Freeman, and Holly Ludgate, *NMC Horizon Report: 2013 Higher Education Edition* (Austin: The New Media Consortium, 2013).

24. Purdue University, "Passport by Purdue University," available at http://www.itap.purdue.edu/studio//passport/, accessed January 15, 2014.

25. "Open Badges," see http://openbadges.org/.

26. HASTAC, "Badges for Lifelong Learning," available at http://hastac.org/groups/badges-lifelong-learning, accessed January 15, 2014.

27. Michele Van Hoeck, "Wikipedia as an Authentic Learning Space," available at http://www.loexconference.org/2013/presentations/LOEX2013_VanHoeck_Slides.pdf, accessed January 15, 2014.

28. Hester Tinti-Kane, "Overcoming Hurdles to Social Media in Education," *Educause Review Online*, (April 1, 2013), available at http://www.educause.edu/ero/article/overcoming-hurdles-social-media-education, accessed January 15, 2014.

29. Jakob Nielsen, "F-Shaped Pattern For Reading Web Content," available at http://www.nngroup.com/articles/f-shaped-pattern-reading-web-content/, accessed January 15, 2014.

30. "National Center on Universal Design for Learning," see, http://www.udlcenter.org/.

31. "From Theory to Practice: UDL "Quick Tips,"Access Project, Colorado State University, available at http://accessproject.colostate.edu/udl/documents/udl_quick_tips.pdf, accessed January 15, 2014.

32. B. A. Frey, L. R. Kearns, and D. K. King, "Quality Matters: Template for an Accessibility Policy for Online Course," Quality Matters Program. 2012. Available at https://www.qualitymatters.org/accessibility-policy-request, accessed January 15, 2014.

33. Frey, Kearns, and King, "Quality Matters."

34. See, "Accessibility Tutorials for Microsoft Products," available at http://www.microsoft.com/enable/training/, accessed on January 15, 2014; Adobe, "Adobe and Accessibility," available at http://www.adobe.com/accessibility.html, accessed January 15, 2014.

35. "Web Accessibility Evaluation Tool," see, http://wave.webaim.org/.

36. Frey, Kearns, and King, "Quality Matters."

37. U.S. Copyright Office, *U.S. Copyright Law. Title 17*, available at http://www.copyright.gov/title17/circ92.pdf, accessed January 15, 2014.

38. Carrie Russell, *Complete Copyright: An Everyday Guide for Librarians,* (Chicago: American Library Association, 2004), 22.

39. Kelly Donohue, "Court Gives Thumbs-up for Use of Thumbnail Pictures Online," *Duke Law & Technology Review* 1, no. 1 (2002): 1–10.

40. See, for example, Columbia Copyright Office, "Columbia Public Domain Resources," available at http://copyright.columbia.edu/copyright/copyright-in-general/public-domain-resources/, accessed on January 15, 2014.

41. "About Creative Commons," available at http://creativecommons.org/about, accessed January 15, 2014.

42. Michael Brewer and ALA Office for Information Technology Policy, "Fair Use Evaluator," available at http://librarycopyright.net/resources/fairuse/, accessed on January 15, 2014.

43. Renee Hobbs, *Copyright Clairty: How Fair Use Supports Digital Learning,* (Thousand Oaks, CA: Corwin and NCTE, 2010).

Chapter Six

Tutorials 101:
Keeping Students Engaged

SCENARIO ONE

An undergraduate student sits down with his laptop, logs in to his library's web site, and begins a tutorial on how to use one of his library's most popular databases. He clicks the start arrow and hears music along with a narrator welcoming him to the tutorial. The student watches a series of slides showing him how to use the database including how to access it from the library homepage, how to use key features, and how to access the full-text of records. The tutorial includes zoomed-in shots to draw attention to important features along with call-out explanatory text. Throughout the tutorial, the student hears a narrator explaining what he is seeing. At the end of the tutorial, the student listens to the narrator read a bulleted list of the key concepts that were covered in the tutorial. The student is then told that he can review the tutorial by clicking the Refresh button.

SCENARIO TWO

An undergraduate student sits down with her laptop and clicks on the link for a tutorial on how to construct effective search strings for library database searching. The tutorial opens with a welcome page that includes an image of a student and brief directions for how to navigate the tutorial. The student clicks the Next arrow and is presented with two scenarios and must choose one to proceed. The student chooses the one that she finds the most interesting and is then presented with a problem that she must help solve. The student is then introduced to Boolean search concepts and must interact with different objects on the screen to construct different search strings. If she places an object on the wrong target, the object jumps back to its original place and the student must choose a different object. With each correct placement, she is awarded more points. At the end of the tutorial, the student is presented with her total points and the option to complete a multiple-choice quiz that will generate a certificate of completion.

The first scenario presents the type of online tutorial that we often see in libraries. They are usually a video or a set of web pages that students click through. Are they effective? The question to ask is: Are they engaging the student? If not, the student will most likely not learn much and not complete the tutorial. The problem with many online tutorials is that they are focused on the content and not the student experience. Instructional design principles tell us that we must start with student learning outcomes and then decide what content we will include that will help us to teach those outcomes. However, we rarely begin the creation process with a discussion of how the student will be motivated to complete the tutorial and their attitude toward it: Are they enjoying the tutorial? Are they engaged with it? Are they actively responding to what is on the screen? Are they feeling that they are learning something as they advance through the tutorial? In this chapter, we begin with a look at passive and active learning and how to write student-centered learning outcomes for tutorials. Next we will explore types of interactivity that you can include in your tutorials and examples of how to make tutorials fun and engaging. We conclude the chapter with a discussion about tutorial software and designing for the mobile environment.

PASSIVE AND ACTIVE LEARNING

The first scenario presented at the beginning of the chapter is an example of passive learning at its worst; it asks the student to do little more than just sit back and watch or listen. A face-to-face classroom in which activities are centered on lectures, readings, and rote memorization is an example of passive, instructor-centered teaching. In contrast, active learning takes place when students are challenged to interact with the content, the instructor, other students, and the course materials.

Unfortunately, many online tutorials are created for passive learning and not active learning. The result is a disengaged student who loses interest quickly even when a video is only four or five minutes long. Although a passive video tutorial can help to introduce new theoretical concepts and activate students' prior learning, it should only account for a brief segment of an online learning object. IL skills require action that students learn

Table 6.1. Active and Passive Learning

Learning Outcome	Passive Learning	Active Learning
Identify different areas in the physical library.	Student looks at a map with clickable buttons of key areas in the library.	Student begins a game with different tasks to complete by going to different areas on the map that will help him or her complete the tasks.
List keywords for a research topic or question.	Student watches a video of another student struggling to find good keywords. Idea bubbles appear as the student on the video comes up with different keywords.	Student is given a topic and must select the correct keywords as they pop up on the screen. Student is given a point for each correct word he or she clicks on.
Evaluate the trustworthiness of different websites.	Student is shown several websites and a narrator that points out what to look for when evaluating a website.	Student is given a topic and links to three different websites. He or she must evaluate each website and choose the one that is most reliable. He or she is then given feedback on his or her choice.
Construct a correctly formatted citation.	Student is shown examples of correct citations for different types of sources.	Student is given a mixed up citation and must put it in the correct order for a particular citation style.

through trial and error, and through doing, not watching. Table 6.1 contrasts an online passive learning activity with an active one for the same student learning outcome.

WRITING STUDENT LEARNING OUTCOMES

The first step in developing a tutorial should start with the writing of the learning outcomes. As you write your learning outcomes, keep in mind what you want your users to *do* and not what you want them to know. Do you want your students to navigate your library's web site successfully? Then your tutorial should have students navigating the web site and not simply watching a video of how it is done. If you want students to be able to list the differences between scholarly and popular sources, providing them with a list of the characteristics of each should suffice. However, if you want students to be able to distinguish between the two, then you want to write student learning outcomes and develop activities where students are actually looking at a source and deciding which type of source it is. (See chapter 3 for best practices in writing active student learning outcomes.)

Many library tutorials attempt to include too many outcomes, and the result is a long and confusing tutorial. Students prefer short tutorials, usually less than three minutes long (for video-type tutorials).[1] It is better to have a series of tutorials students can choose from rather than presenting them with a long tutorial that attempts to cover too much. With self-paced interactive tutorials, it is difficult to measure how long a student will take to complete it because times will vary greatly between students. However, we recommend starting with only three measurable outcomes and adding more later if needed. The outcomes for one tutorial we created on searching more effectively are listed below:

Upon completion of the tutorial the student will be able to:

- Generate related keywords based on a given topic
- Describe how to use the Boolean operator *AND*
- Combine keywords correctly with the Boolean operator *AND*

In this tutorial, the student is first introduced to the concept of *AND* through a brief reading. They are then asked to select keywords and related terms for a few different topics, and the student is given feedback on their selection. Next, the student is shown how to combine words with *AND*. The student is then presented with keywords, related terms, and the word *AND* and must create different search strings with them. Lastly, the student is presented with a series of multiple choice questions to assess their learning. After completing this tutorial, we decided to add the concept of *OR* because it was still relatively short. Although there are other related concepts we would like students to know, we felt that adding more would not enhance student learning but rather overwhelm them with too much information.

BUILDING INTERACTIVITY

Numerous researchers and educators cite the importance of interactivity in tutorials.[2] Mayer and Chandler found that even the simplest form of interaction had a positive impact on user retention and transfer of learning.[3] In their 2001 study on simple user interactions and deep understanding of the material, they found significant differences in the transfer of learning between students who viewed presentations in their entirety and those who were able to click through the material at their own pace. Even this simplest form of interaction allows the student to interact with the content in a more meaningful manner. Chien and Chang found that the more meaningful the interaction, the more students learn.[4] They created three types of tutorials to teach a basic scientific concept, the use of an Abney Level (a surveying measuring instrument): one with a static image and text, one with images and text where students could control the pacing of the tutorial, and one with images, text, pacing, and student manipulation of an onscreen Abney level. The researchers found that students who viewed the third type of tutorial performed significantly better than the other two groups.

Interactivity is the main element that sets apart passive, often boring tutorials from effective and engaging ones, but there is little consensus on what constitutes interactivity in a tutorial. Some online tutorial designers consider navigation as interactivity whereas others consider a multiple-choice test at the end of a tutorial as interactive. There are different levels of interactivity from simple interaction, self-pacing options, to more meaningful interactions such as manipulating objects on a screen. We classify interactions into the four categories starting from the simplest form of interaction to the most complex.

1. Navigation: This level of interactivity serves to take the student to a different place in the tutorial. It can be in the form of a clickable menu, arrows, video controls, or a clickable image. This is the simplest level of interactivity and does not require much thought or reflection, although there is a physical response to the tutorial.
2. Information: This type of interactivity serves as a way for content to be communicated to the student. It can be in the form of a video the student can advance through, text, or an on-screen character speaking. The student can access the content through a number of ways including hovering over an object, clicking on an image, or following a link to another slide or an external source.
3. Application: This is the level where true interactivity occurs. It is both a physical (clicking, dragging, and dropping) and mental response to an object on a screen. This type of interactivity asks the learner to apply new knowledge and practice new skills. It can be in the form of drag and drops, clickable objects, and quizzing features such as hot spots or multiple choice. Although this type of interactivity can take the form of a quiz, it should not be designed to assess student learning, but rather be used as practice and application of skills. Figure 6.1 shows this type of interaction from our tutorial How to Search Effectively. After a brief reading about keywords and related terms, the student must place the terms into appropriate circles. The student must correctly place all of the terms before being allowed to continue.

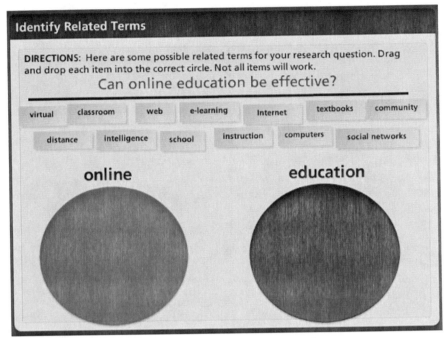

Identify Related Terms

DIRECTIONS: Here are some possible related terms for your research question. Drag and drop each item into the correct circle. Not all items will work.

Can online education be effective?

virtual   classroom   web   e-learning   Internet   textbooks   community

distance   intelligence   school   instruction   computers   social networks

online

education

Figure 6.1.   Tutorial with Application of Skills as a Drag and Drop

4. Manipulation: This is the most immersive type of online interactivity, and it is the most difficult to design. This type of interactivity is highly customized and asks the student to manipulate different areas on the screen to both apply their knowledge and learn from their input. For the user to be truly engaged in this type of activity, they must respond to the tutorial and the tutorial must respond back to them in a manner specific to their input. Video games, online gaming, and three-dimensional simulations are some examples of this type of interactivity. Many medical schools have online tutorials in which students can look at and manipulate different parts of the human body to complete a set of tasks.

BUILDING ENGAGEMENT

The Fun Theory

A few years ago Volkswagen carried out a series of experiments based on *the fun theory*; the idea that people can be motivated to do something if you make it fun. Each experiment was filmed and many became hits on YouTube. In one experiment workers in a Swedish subway station covered the stairs with large working piano keys. The video shows folks of all ages choosing the stairs over the escalator right next to them. Some folks even go up and down the stairs a few times. The video informs us that 66 percent more people than normal chose the stairs over the escalator. What if we adopted this fun theory when developing information literacy tutorials for our libraries? Would students be more motivated to complete them?

When we set out to transform our instruction for an online audience, we developed many tutorials around this idea of fun to motivate students. Most of our IL tutorials are created for use in courses in which we can assign them and more easily track student usage. However, many of our tutorials are also repurposed for general use and accessed through our library homepage. We have no way of ensuring that these students complete them. Students are most often motivated by grades, but if there is no grade at stake, we must find a different way to motivate them. Making tutorials fun and engaging gives us more assurance that our tutorials will be viewed and students will learn from them. After all, many students spend hours playing video games when the only real reward is fun. Why not transfer this same idea to our tutorials? As Marc Prensky, one of the early proponents of using games in learning states: "Learning, as great teachers have known throughout the ages, does not feel like work when you're having fun."[5] There are a number of ways to make a tutorial fun:

- Include humor and drama: One of the best tutorials we have seen tackles a not-so-fun subject, manager training. Most management trainings consist of reading the company handbook followed by answering a few questions. In the online environment this may include watching a video. Pretty boring stuff, but the tutorial designers made it fun by adding drama in the form of a possible office romance and humor in the form of strange behaviors from office workers who were possibly drinking on the job. The result was a tutorial that was both fun to do and where the user learned about the company's managerial policies.
- Turn it into a game: Students spend hours playing video games for little reward save for enjoyment and gratification. What drives them is the challenge of not losing, the ability to get a higher score, and the improvement of their own skills. This same type of motivation can be added to tutorials by adding points to a score, imposing a time limit and adding a ticking clock, and asking students to complete a challenge with consequences for a wrong answer.
- Add characters: Characters help to add a sense of personalization to an otherwise flat tutorial. Many software programs have a range of characters that can be easily placed into a tutorial and customized. You can change how the character looks and give them a persona from a humorous laid-back student

to a serious A+ student. Additionally, you can make the characters react to student input by cheering them on and encouraging them to try again. Characters can also be used to help navigate the student through a tutorial.

MAKE IT REAL

One of the basic principles of adult education theory is the need to offer students instruction that is immediately relevant and applicable. Adult learners, including college students, have a world of prior experiences and knowledge that they can draw from. Similarly, students taking an IL course need to see how the tutorial they are watching and the skills they are gaining from it can be used once they complete the tutorial. Most students want to take as little time as possible to go through the tutorial. Additionally, because of their prior knowledge of searching, they also want to figure it out on their own. To make tutorials immediately relevant for students, they should be as authentic as possible. Here are some tips for making tutorials more relevant:

- Use problem-based scenarios: Students search for information to solve a problem (i.e., to fill an information need, to access the full-text of an article, to locate a primary resource). Designing a tutorial that centers on a problem or scenario that the student needs to figure out as opposed to one that is designed around the content allows students to apply their skills to the type of situation they may find themselves in later. Here is the wording from one of our tutorials on using primary resources:

  > After some reading, Rainbow decides to focus on the art of the 1960s' peace movement. She finds the poster shown here but is not sure she can use it. She needs to determine whether it is a primary or secondary source. You can help her by examining the source more closely. Hover over the image to see more information about it. Once you have examined it, decide if it is a primary or secondary source.

- Individualize instruction: Most of our students come to us with varying levels of IL and from all disciplines across campus. As such we need to find a balance between helping the lower-level student while still engaging the higher-level student. One way we do this is by offering students a choice of the type of activity they would like to start with. For example, in many of our tutorials we let the student decide if they want to start with a background reading, a game, or an assessment. We also create different topic areas the student can choose from. The student learning outcomes are the same but the student can decide if they want to learn in the context of a topic related to literature, history, or science.

- Include repeated practice of skills: Showing a student how to search the library's catalog to locate a book chapter and then having a student answer a question on how to do it does not mean the student will be able to perform this same task later on. Many IL skills are learned and mastered through repetitive practice, and tutorials should offer students a place to practice these skills repeatedly. Additionally, tutorials offer students a place where they can practice skills in a safe environment where mistakes do not have terrible consequences. In many of our tutorials we build activities where students are able to practice the same skills a number of times.

- Use authentic tasks: Because most tutorials can only simulate what a student will need to do when searching a catalog or evaluating a web site, it is difficult to give students real hands-on experience in a tutorial. However, tasks can be created that look and feel like the "real thing." For example if you need students to evaluate the authority of a web site, your tutorial can include screenshots with different parts of a web site. You can then include guided instructions for what to look at followed by questions that ask the student to evaluate the web site. The use of frames in a browser can also be used to have students complete tasks. Our library developed such a tutorial that we called the Guide on the Side (see Figure 6.2). The Guide on the Side can be used with any live web page and offers students the chance to manipulate the web page according to instructions on one side of the screen. This type of tutorial was developed partially to

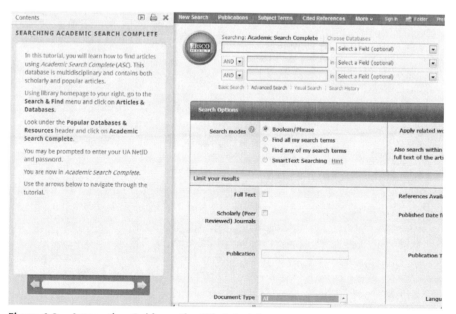

Figure 6.2.   Interactive Guide on the Side tutorial

give students the type of hands-on practice we do not commonly see in screencast database tutorials.[6]

- Provide more details only as needed: As mentioned, our students have varying degrees of information literacy know-how. One strategy we use to help students at all levels is to offer additional information using help buttons the students can access if they feel they need more help to complete a task. These buttons can be in the form of images, FAQs, or buttons students can click on and access additional information. In our Finding Library Materials tutorial, we show students a number of different results they may come across when searching the catalog and then ask them which service they would use to access the material. If students need additional help to figure out what to do, they can access definitions of different services.

MAKE IT EFFECTIVE

Using Principles of Multimedia Instruction

All of the strategies and tips discussed help to make a tutorial more effective. However, a tutorial that is engaging, fun, and realistic can still fail to teach the student. Most often this occurs when principles of multimedia learning are violated. Most widely attributed to Richard E. Mayer and supported through empirical research, these principles grew out of theories of cognitive load.[7] Cognitive load theory states that when overwhelmed with excessive input, the brain's ability to process information becomes overloaded and learning ceases to take place.[8] The principles explained here are some of the most commonly misused principles that we see in tutorials:

- Do not use audio, text, and graphics: Have you ever attended a PowerPoint presentation where the speaker shows a slide with text and then proceeds to read the text while interjecting additional commentary as they read? Chances are you could not read the text and listen to the presenter at the same time. Figure 6.3 shows an example of a common tutorial where the text and the spoken narration are presented simultaneously. It is impossible to read both pieces of text together. Similarly, it is difficult to read and listen to duplicative narration at the same time.

  By far, this is the principle we most often see ignored in tutorials. Presenting students the same information as both text and audio, requires an overwhelming amount of work on the cognitive areas of the brain. Mayer and Moreno explain that the brain has two different channels to process information: an auditory processing channel and a visual processing channel.[9] When one channel is presented with two visual inputs (an animation

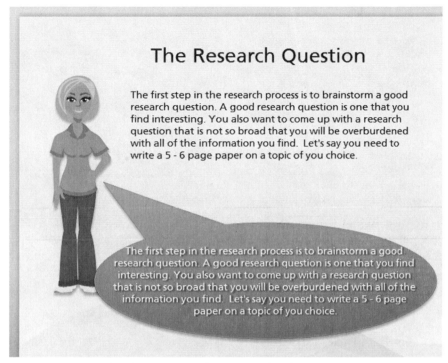

Figure 6.3. Tutorial with Both Redundant Text and Spoken Narration

and text), the channel becomes overloaded and learning does not take place. Similarly, with on-screen text and unnecessary narration, the brain becomes overloaded. Clark and Meyer discuss several studies that looked at the use of animations, narration, and on-screen text and their effect on learning.[10] In each study, students who were not presented with redundant material, as in the case of text and repeated narration, outperformed students who were presented with more media. As Clark and Meyer explain, in e-learning, less is often more.[11]

Many librarians we talk with tell us that they must use both audio and text to be in compliance with Americans with Disabilities Act guidelines. If you must include both audio and text in a tutorial you should make them optional. For example, you can include a closed captioning button where the text can be read to the student if they wish to hear it.

• Use graphics that matter: Visuals are common in library tutorials but they are often overused or incorrectly used. Learning style theories show that students learn in different ways; some learn better visually, others learn better when information is presented in an audio form. However, with many concepts, all students will learn better when there is a visual representation that helps to explain the concept.

Question 1

Choose the best database for the research
question below:

What is the effect of music in the classroom on
elementary students' math test scores?

A. ERIC
B. Web of Science
C. PubMed
D. RefWorks

Figure 6.4.   Tutorial with Gratuitous Decorative Image

Although visuals can help improve learning, they can also distract from
it. We have seen numerous tutorials in which images are included to fill
up space or make the slide look more appealing. Figure 6.4 shows an image that has been inserted for purely decorative purposes. Clark and Meyer
found that these types of decorative images do not help learning and in
many cases often distract from the learning.[12]

To reduce cognitive load when using images, explanatory labels should
be placed next to the images instead of below, above them, or on another
page. Figure 6.5 shows ineffective use of labeling that puts extra burden on
the student and can lead to cognitive overload. Figure 6.6 shows a better
use of labeling with interactive buttons for explanatory text.

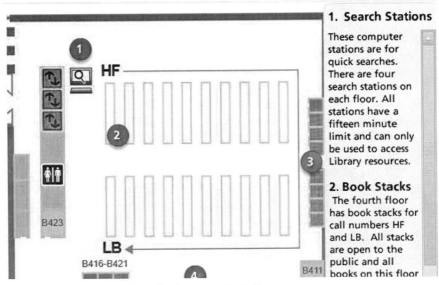

Figure 6.5.   Tutorial with Ineffective Use of Labeling

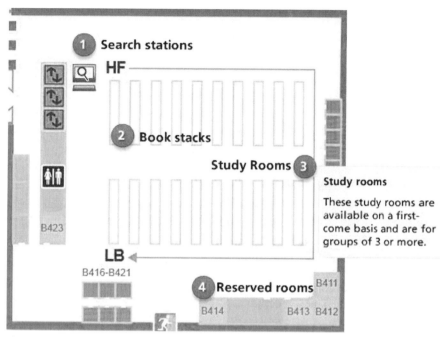

Figure 6.6. Tutorial with More Effective Use of Labeling

- Use sparse text: Skimming and scanning is a common way to read any type of digital text. One web site usability study found that only 16 percent of subjects read an entire page word for word. Of course students will need to read some text to understand certain concepts and to follow instructions. However, when possible, text should be kept to a minimum. Jakob Nielsen, a well-known usability consultant suggests using bullet points, highlighted keywords, and including only one idea per paragraph to make web pages more readable.[13] In our tutorials we also break text into smaller chunks on a page, place a short amount of text on each slide, and make some nonessential text optional to read.

CHOOSING THE SOFTWARE

Ideally, quality online learning objects, whether they consist of a short how-to tutorial or a series of tutorials on basic research principles, are developed by a team of librarians, programmers, instructional designers, web developers, and content experts. However, reduced resources force librarians to develop learning objects either on their own or in partnership with a single programmer. Often this lone-ranger model of tutorial development results in a rushed learning object with a short life span because updates require additional scarce resources and additional collaboration. Additionally, many librarians have little time and inadequate programming skills to develop quality tutorials and must usually turn to screencasting software programs that are passive in nature. However, the introduction of rapid e-learning software programs is making it easier for librarians to create quality tutorials that typically require programmers or web developers.

Rapid e-learning tools have allowed educators and corporate trainers with few skills in web development or design to create professional, engaging, and interactive learning objects. Rapid e-learning programs are authoring tools that produce rich-media tutorials in Flash or HTML format. Although relatively well-known in the business sector, libraries have yet to widely embrace rapid e-learning programs. These programs place the development of online instructional materials in the hands of librarians as opposed to programmers or web developers. Work time is lessened and learning curves are diminished because the work is often done within PowerPoint or via the manipulation of Flash templates. Rapid e-learning tools that allow for the creation of asynchronous learning objects include Articulate Storyline and Presenter, Adobe Captivate, Lectora, and Raptivity. These tools allow librarians and educators with few technology skills to develop quality learning objects much more quickly than traditional creation software that often requires some level of programming. Additionally because they are so easy to use, development can start immediately without the need to dedicate a lot of time to storyboarding. We often take a prototype approach to tutorial design where we create a skeleton tutorial and then add elements as needed. A list of some factors to consider when choosing a content authoring program follows:

- Cost: Most programs cost from the low hundreds to more than $3,000 per license
- Learning Curve: The more customizable features a program has, the more difficult it will be to learn. Some programs such as Adobe Captivate have a much steeper learning curve than products from Articulate.
- Interactive features: clickable buttons, drag and drops, hovers, text input boxes, etc.
- Quizzing features: multiple choice, hot spot, true/false, short answer, etc.
- SCORM compliant
- Americans with Disabilities Act compliant

- Templates and easy customization of templates
- Video embedding
- Audio creation and editing functions
- Graphics that look professional
- Technology support options and training
- Mobile device output
- Web- or cloud-based platform

DEVELOPING FOR MOBILE

With the ongoing increase in the use of mobile devices, developing tutorials that are mobile friendly can no longer be an afterthought. Many software programs now include options to publish in HTML5 or apps such as the Articulate app that allows for easy viewing of tutorials created with any of its suite of tools. However, creating a tutorial with mobile-friendly software does not guarantee success. Just as the digital environment calls for different pedagogical and design approaches, mobile learning has its own set of rules for what works. Tutorial elements may look and feel different on a mobile device, and many tutorial features that allow for interactivity do not work on a mobile device. For example, hovering over images and buttons, and drag-and-drop features do not work on mobile devices. Additionally, if buttons and other clickable features are not large enough, they will be difficult to see and touch. Thus, making a tutorial accessible on a tablet or a phone is not just an issue of the output but also of the design. It is quite possible that you will have to design two tutorials, one for mobile and one for the desktop. However, advances in responsive web design will allow for easier accessibility between devices without having to resort to the creation of different tutorials.

KNOW THIS . . .

- Screencast video tutorials are forms of passive learning that fail to engage students.
- Engagement in a tutorial must be a priority.
- There are a number of ways to make a tutorial engaging including making it fun and adding interactions.
- There are several levels of interactivity, and navigation is the simplest level.
- For a tutorial to be effective, it must include multiple practice opportunities and application of skills.

- Studies in educational psychology show that too much media in a tutorial creates cognitive overload.
- Rapid e-learning tools can help you design interactive tutorials without the need for programming skills.

NOTES

1. Melissa Bowles-Terry, Merinda Kaye Hensley, and Lisa Janicke Hinchliffe, "Best Practices for Online Video Tutorials: A Study of Student Preferences and Understanding," *Communications in Information Literacy*, 4, no. 1 (2010): 17–28.

2. Cecile Bianco, "Online Tutorials: Tips from the Literature," *Library Philosophy and Practice* 8 (2005), available at http://www.webpages.uidaho.edu/~mbolin/bianco2.htm, accessed January 16, 2014; Nancy H. Dewald, "Web-Based Library Instruction: What Is Good Pedagogy?" *Information Technology and Libraries* 18, no. 1 (1999): 26–31; Arthur Chickering and Stephen C. Ehrmann. "Implementing the Seven Principles: Technology as Lever," *AAHE Bulletin* (October 1996): 3–6; Jim Henry and Jeff Meadows, "An Absolutely Riveting Online Course: Nine Principles for Excellence in Web-Based Teaching," *Canadian Journal of Learning and Technology* 34, no. 1 (2008), available at http://www.cjlt.ca/index.php/cjlt/article/view/179/177, accessed January 16, 2014

3. Richard E. Mayer and Paul Chandler, "When Learning Is Just a Click Away: Does Simple User Interaction Foster Deeper Understanding of Multimedia Messages?" *Journal of Educational Psychology* 93, no. 2 (2001): 390–397.

4. Yu-Ta Chien and Chun-Yen Chang, "Comparison of Different Instructional Multimedia Designs for Improving Student Science-Process Skill Learning," *Journal of Science Education and Technology* 21 (2012): 106–113.

5. Marc Prensky, "Computer Games and Learning: Digital Game-Based Learning," in *Handbook of Computer Games Studies*, edited by J. Raessens and J. Goldstein (Cambridge, MA: The MIT Press, 2005), 59–79.

6. Leslie Sult, Yvonne Mery, Rebecca Blakiston Blakiston, and Elizabeth Kline, "A New Approach to Online Database Instruction: Developing the Guide on the Side." *Reference Services Review* 41, no. 1 (2013): 125–133.

7. Richard E. Mayer, ed. *The Cambridge Handbook of Multimedia Learning.* (New York: University of Cambridge, 2005).

8. John Sweller. *Instructional Design in Technical Areas.* (Camberwell, VIC, Australia: ACER Press, 1999).

9. Richard E. Mayer and Roxana Moreno, "Nine Ways to Reduce Cognitive Load in Multimedia Learning," *Educational Psychologist* 39, no. 1 (2003): 43–52.

10. Ruth C. Clark and Richard E. Mayer, *E-learning and the Science of Instruction: Proven Guidelines for Consumers and Designers of Multimedia Learning*, 3rd. San Francisco, CA: Pfeiffer, 2011.

11. Ibid.

12. Ibid.

13. Jakob Nielsen. "Concise, SCANNABLE, and Objective: How to Write for the Web." *Nielsen Norman Group.* 1997. Available at http://www.nngroup .com/articles/concise-scannable-and-objective-how-to-write-for-the-web/, accessed January 16, 2014.

SUGGESTED READING

Allen, Michael W. *Michael Allen's Guide to e-Learning : Building Interactive, Fun, and Effective Learning Programs for any Company.* Hoboken, NJ: John Wiley, 2003.

Wroblewski, Luke. *Mobile First.* New York: A Book Apart, 2011.

Chapter Seven

Assignments 101: Making It Real, Related, and Rewarding

INTRODUCTION

One of the author's first questions on the reference desk was from a junior urban studies major who needed help with his paper. "Can you help me with my citations for an assignment? Like putting them all there?" he asked. She followed him to his computer and he showed her his completed paper on gentrification in large cities. He informed her that now he just needed to add some citations in between the paragraphs. She asked how many sources he had collected and read, and he admitted that he had not read any of the many laid out before him. He had not read a single book or article yet he was able to write a lengthy paper on a fairly difficult topic, and now he needed to figure out how to include the minimum number of citations the assignment called for.

Sadly, this is how many students approach research assignments today. Usually they wait until the last minute to start their assignment and then only have time to write. Actually researching the topic is an afterthought. As Fister notes,[1]

> . . . the trouble is they don't read them, or they read only enough to find a useful quote, or they choose sources that are not particularly insightful ones, or their paper becomes merely a description of the sources they've found with little analysis or original thought. A more sophisticated mistake is to seek out only sources that support a previously-held belief.

Fister, along with Holliday and Rogers, note that this emphasis on sources is partially a result of instructors and librarians' emphasis on using the term *sources* and not on research or information.[2] Much of our instruction in IL courses and in one-shot sessions is spent on developing discrete searching skills and using a few databases where we emphasize locating sources rather than getting to know a topic. Similarly, a common IL course final assignment is an annotated bibliography where finding and listing sources is emphasized.

Much of this superficial use of sources can be avoided by creating better assignments. In this chapter, we look at how to create assignments that are meaningful, that build on critical-thinking skills, and that ask students to interact and react to the sources they find. We also discuss the benefits of assignments, best practices in assignment creation, and offer samples of assignments from our courses in the chapter appendices.

ASSIGNMENTS: MORE THAN BUSY WORK

Assignments can be quite time consuming to create and grade, but the payoff in terms of student learning is worth the effort. The greatest benefit of an assignment is that it offers students opportunities to practice what they have learned in a meaningful and practical way. Skills such as those acquired in an IL course will have more relevance to students when they can see their immediate applicability. Through an assignment, students can see that what they learned through readings, tutorials, and lectures can be used in the "real world."

Assignments can also help students apply what they have learned to a new experience or situation. This type of assignment could be as simple as assigning students to locate information on a topic outside their discipline and having them reflect on their search process, or as complex as a collaborative group project based on a case study. Smaller, mini-assignments or exercises can be used to prepare students for the final, bigger project or assignment.

Assignments also help students to gain confidence in their skills as researchers. In our graduate course, we have three assignments in which students use their search topic to locate and export references into RefWorks or EndNote. At the end of the third assignment, not only have students collected references for their research, but they have also experienced exporting references from a variety of disciplinary databases. They have learned to use library help guides, as well as vendor tutorials when they get stuck. Many have used the chat reference service to get help when we were not available to answer their questions. Most importantly, they have gained self-assurance in their ability to use citation management software for storing and managing references for their research and coursework.

Assignments are part of the assessment process that provides evidence of student learning and performance. In addition to getting a grade, feedback from an assignment helps students validate what they have learned and what areas of performance they need to improve. As instructors, an assignment provides an evaluation about how well the learning materials and activities supported student success. It also helps to identify problems with the assignment so that changes, such as clearer instructions, simplification or reduction of tasks, or a better alignment with the learning outcomes can be made. As is the case with many aspects of online teaching, assignments are never quite "done," and there is always room for improvement.

CREATING MEANINGFUL ASSIGNMENTS

The Foundation for Critical Thinking defines critical thinking as "the intellectually disciplined process of actively and skillfully conceptualizing, applying, analyzing, synthesizing, and/or evaluating information gathered from, or generated by, observation, experience, reflection, reasoning, or communication, as a guide to belief and action."[3] Having students search for sources and then create an annotated bibliography does not support this idea of critical thinking. Unless students are asked to interact with, digest, and learn from the sources they find, they will not be spurred to any type of "belief and action." The overall goal of an IL assignment and of an IL course, for that matter, should be to help students become fluent not only in the research process but also in a chosen or assigned research topic. Unfortunately much of our IL teaching has focused on the former.

Initially our undergraduate course put a great deal of emphasis on extending students searching skills and familiarizing them with several information resources in the library. Through our final project, an annotated bibliography assignment, we soon came to the realization that even after finishing a semester-long IL course, students were still struggling to make sense of what they were finding and using it in their papers effectively. Their bibliographies showed a wide range of information sources from web sites to scholarly research articles, all correctly formatted to MLA specifications; however, a deeper look at their sources revealed some issues: many sources were not quite relevant to their topic; others were much too scientific for an undergraduate paper; others lacked currency; and many lacked any authority or credibility.

To place more of an emphasis on critical-thinking skills and the use of sources, we redesigned the curriculum to focus on developing students' fluency in a topic before they begin looking for sources. Instead of having students create their own research question at the start of the course, we now have them choose from among four research questions we have created:

- College sports: Should college athletes be better compensated financially?
- Gun rights: Should people be allowed to carry guns on college campuses?
- Obesity: Is government legislation an effective way to fight obesity?
- Sex Education: Are abstinence-only sex education programs effective at preventing teen pregnancy?

Students spend the first four weeks of class getting to know their chosen research question through several assigned readings and short exercises that focus on the content of the readings. They spend this time familiarizing themselves with the nuances of the topic and the different viewpoints. During this reading portion of the course, students learn about and read different types of information sources including books, scholarly journals, and web sites. Ultimately, they come to care more about their topic and develop a fluency in it that will allow them to better search for and critically evaluate what they find.

This emphasis on finding out more about their topic and not on locating sources has allowed us to create assignments that focus on critical-thinking and reading skills and that lead to more comprehensive and substantial work. In their book on creating assignments for IL classes, Burkhardt, MacDonald, and Rathemacher describe an excellent cumulative assignment, the Paper Trail Project that asks students to show how they conducted the research, what they know about their topic, and how they can use their sources to sustain their argument.[4] This is a long project that would be best suited for a full three-credit course, but it can be easily adapted to fit courses that grant fewer credits.

BEST PRACTICES IN ASSIGNMENT DEVELOPMENT

A focus on developing critical thinking and reading is a first step in creating effective assignments, but there are many other elements that are needed to ensure a well-designed, engaging assignment. In the face-to-face classroom, you can pass out an assignment and answer any clarification questions on the spot. However, in the online course, you will need to anticipate these questions and incorporate them into your assignments ahead of time because students cannot get their questions answered immediately. In our undergraduate course, students often wait until the last minute to look at an assignment, and often it is too late to contact us and wait for an answer, so they must start the assignment without being entirely clear on what they are being asked to do. The following best practices offer concrete methods to ensure that students get the most out of assignments.

- Give frequent assignments to help students keep up with the content and to provide them with continuous feedback throughout the course. The frequency of the assignments will be dependent on the size of the class and your own workload constraints.
- The assignment should align with the unit learning outcomes. Present the learning outcomes at the beginning of the assignment to provide context for the students. Give a brief explanation about why they are being asked to carry out the assignment and a brief description of what they will be doing.
- Communicate your expectations for the assignment in the form of a rubric or criteria for excellent work so that students will understand what is required of them to successfully complete the assignment. (Creating rubrics will be addressed in the next chapter on assessment.) For each question include the number of points awarded for a complete answer. Fenton and Watkins recommend providing exemplary and unacceptable examples of assignments so that students have a clear understanding of what excellence looks like.[5] Provide clear instructions on how to carry out the assignment, especially if there are a number of tasks, or technological processes, such as creating an account in a new web application or uploading completed assignments to the LMS. Ask a colleague to review your assignment instructions to see if they are clear and well organized.
- It can be difficult to keep track of assignments and even harder when students forget to put their names on it. Although this point may seem trivial, you should include an area on the assignment for students to put their names. Before we began doing this and reminding students of it, we would constantly receive assignments and papers with no names on them, which ended up taking more time to match the assignment with the student's name.
- Be available to answer questions about the assignment or provide a discussion topic where students can get help from each other. Another useful strategy is to create an FAQ that provides answers to commonly asked questions.
- Undergraduates need more guidance in assignments than graduate students. Pallof suggests using "sequential learning tasks"[6] in which students start with a familiar type of assignment that includes a great deal of direction, such as an assignment that requires students to locate an article on a topic and provide a summary. Then move on to a more open-ended assignment that does not include as much direction where students need to tap into different learning modes, such as evaluating brief passages of text for plagiarism and being able to paraphrase a paragraph.
- Make assignments progressively challenging. Use Bloom's Taxonomy of learning objectives for the cognitive domain to create a variety of assignments from *describing* a concept, through *analyzing* or *critiquing*, through *creating* something new based on the learning.[7]

- Offer students choices in assignments that are due at different times during the course but are worth the same number of points.[8] Kaplowitz recommends this option for learner-centered assignments to give students more flexibility and responsibility for completing assignments that works well with their course schedule and in a manner that they are most interested. Among the suggested assignment types, Kaplowitz lists creating a blog, writing a review of a book or a web site, or interviewing an expert on a topic.[9]

- Provide prompt grading and individualized feedback so that students have time to reflect on their performance and can incorporate their learning into subsequent assignments and tests. In our graduate course, where the number of students is manageable, we include individualized feedback for each assignment. This is a great way to make connections with students and to let them know that you are interested in their learning.[10] Manage students' expectations for grading and feedback by including this information in the syllabus. The turnaround time should be within a week of the assignment submission date; ideally at least two days after the due date.

- Allow students to make revisions to their assignment based on feedback.[11] Although this will create more work and certainly wouldn't work well in a large class, this will increase student engagement with the material and improve overall learning.

- To improve the effectiveness of your assignments, ask students for feedback about the length of assignments, whether they are too time consuming or complex.[12] If students are overwhelmed with an assignment, it can lead to cheating.

- Well-designed assignments that are aligned with learning outcomes are not easy to create. Successful assignments require several revisions both during the course planning and development phase and after the assignments are used each semester. Do all the assignments yourself before assigning them to your students. This is a great way to learn about issues, such as missing steps in instructions or dead hyperlinks that you can correct beforehand.[13] Also, you will be better able to make modifications to the assignment where you experienced difficulties, or to make suggestions to students about the challenges they might come across with the assignment.

Avoiding Plagiarism

Plagiarism and cheating are not exclusive to the online course, but the medium does make it easier. To lessen the instances of plagiarism, it should be discussed early in the course. You should not rely solely on the plagiarism warning you included in your syllabus; instead, bring it up before the first assignment or exam, and then again whenever an assignment is due. A unit on plagiarism should provide students with information about what constitutes plagiarism, what it looks like, and how to avoid it by paraphrasing and citing correctly. In our undergraduate course, we have students view a tutorial on avoiding plagiarism by using sources correctly, and then discussing different scenarios where plagiarism may have occurred. In our graduate course, we provide constant feedback on the correct use of a citation style chosen by the student.

Creating assignments that are more plagiarism-proof is perhaps the best solution to preventing plagiarism. You should create assignments that have a number of parts that build on each other, often referred to as scaffolding. Providing the structure to create a research project in pieces makes it less likely that students will panic at the last minute when a big project is due and turn to the Internet for a quick and easy solution.[14] Scaffolding assignments, especially writing assignments, provides opportunities for the instructor to learn an individual student's writing style and vocabulary. This makes it easier to detect plagiarism if a student's writing style is not similar to previous submissions. Another option is to assign topics that are focused on a specific current topic that may not be so easily found in Internet paper mills. It is important to frequently change the assignment topic so that assignments are not handed down from one class to another.[15]

There is also the option of using a plagiarism detection program, such as TurnitIn or SafeAssign, that are integrated into the LMS. If you decide to use a plagiarism detection program, take the time to learn how to use the program and how to correctly review the resulting reports.[16] In addition, be prepared when a plagiarism incident occurs by being familiar with campus policies and procedures for dealing with plagiarism.

COLLABORATIVE ASSIGNMENTS

Today's student is most likely familiar with group and project work as it has become the norm in many primary and secondary classrooms, and this type of work has a number of benefits for both students and instructors. Students benefit from working with a diverse group of students with potentially different viewpoints; they learn how to work as a team; and as part of a team of peers, they may be more motivated to do better and complete their work on time. Additionally, collaborative assignments can help students gain the skills highly sought after by employers today.[17] Collaborative work can also help alleviate time spent on grading because instructors do not have to grade individual assignments. All of these benefits hold true for the online course as well, and with the rise of cloud- and web-based social collaboration tools such as wikis, Skype, and Google Drive, online group work has never been easier.

Although collaborative group work and assignments offer a number of benefits for both students and instructors, you should be deliberate and careful in their design. According to the Eberly Center for Teaching Excellence and Educational Innovation at Carnegie Mellon, "simply assigning group work is no guarantee that these goals will be achieved. In fact, group projects can—and often do—backfire badly when they are not designed, supervised, and assessed in a way that promotes meaningful teamwork and deep collaboration."[18] You must also make sure that you design group projects that have multiple components where students can easily divide the work among themselves. A case-study project allows for this more meaningful type of group work. In a case-study example, students work together to figure out the course of action that should be taken for a particular problem. For example, one of the authors created IL tutorials for a nutrition sciences course where groups of students were asked to come up with a dietary plan for a newly admitted patient. Students were required to research the illness the patient had, the drugs they were taking and any possible interactions, and conduct research into the effectiveness of different treatment options to create a specialized diet for the patient. They also needed to present their findings to the rest of the class and include a lengthy bibliography. Although these types of case studies are most often discipline specific, they can be easily adapted for a more general IL course.

Worcester Polytechnic Institute's web pages on group work offer a number of great student tips including exchanging contact information with other students and dividing up group responsibilities.[19] Such a list of tips may work well with graduate students who tend to be more self-directed. However, for the undergraduate student, these tips should be incorporated into the design of the assignment as sub-tasks. As Kaplowitz explains, "the instructor must be vigilant in keeping groups on track and on schedule." [20] For example, as part of the assignment, you can ask students to send e-mail messages to one another where they can exchange personal information and introduce themselves. As another preliminary task, you can ask students to send you a list of the group participants and their roles. These smaller tasks and checking in on them will help to keep students on track.

As effective as collaborative group assignments can be, you may be hesitant to implement them in the online course, and there are plenty of reasons to proceed cautiously with online group work. Group assignments can be quite time intensive to both create and implement. As Kaplowitz explains, "the truth is that using collaborative group work requires the instructor to keep an even tighter rein on things."[21] This "tighter rein" means much more time spent communicating with students on a daily or weekly basis. Although beneficial to them, group work is not always viewed favorably by students.[22]

If you are hesitant to create and use a group project in your course, you can include collaborative elements of group work on a smaller scale by providing opportunities for peer review of assignments. This promotes student-student interaction and engages students with the criteria for successful completion of the assignment. Especially in an online course in which students may feel isolated from each other, peer review allows students to validate their work against another student's work. Also, it provides another viewpoint on their work other than the instructor.[23] In our graduate student course, the final project is a research portfolio of work that has been completed during the course. There are two assignments during the course in which students demonstrate their progress on the research portfolio before their final end-of-course submission. In the second assignment, students are paired to provide written feedback on each others' portfolio and are graded on their review. Students are asked to provide feedback on how well the portfolio, which is presented in a web site, meets the research portfolio requirements. This includes both the presentation of information as well as the completeness of the entries. Students have told us that they appreciate the opportunity to receive feedback from peers and to gauge how well they are doing on their final project.

WORKLOAD MANAGEMENT

Assignments that require a great deal of review and feedback are often the most effective for student learning. However, class size does influence the types of assignments that are feasible in the online course and there must be a balance between interaction and workload issues. As noted by Ko and Rossen, "You can't have a high level of individual student-instructor interaction in an online class of 40 or more students."[24] With more than forty students, Ko and Rossen advise designing group projects where you are interacting with groups, not individuals. Also having a teaching assistant with a class size of forty students or more is highly recommended to assist in communication and grading assignments.[25]

We were able to significantly reduce the instructor workload in our undergraduate course when we redesigned the curriculum to focus more on the research question and getting to know it and less on immediately finding sources (see this chapter's section on creating meaningful assignments for more details). Having students choose from a list of research questions instead of having them formulate their own question has significantly reduced the time spent on grading. When students were required to create their own research question, the instructor had to spend a great deal of time helping the student narrow or expand their question. As mentioned previously, this was quite difficult to do in the online environment. The instructor also had to potentially evaluate the sources every student located and answered questions about. Thus, for one assignment in a course with twenty-five students the instructor had to read and evaluate potentially twenty-five different articles. With the list of just four possible research questions to choose from, we were able to develop questions that asked students to more critically evaluate their sources while reducing the time spent on grading. A limited number of research questions have also allowed us to develop more detailed rubrics which make grading significantly easier.

KNOW THIS . . .

- Design assignments that provide evidence of students being able to meet the learning outcomes. Include the learning outcomes in the assignment to provide students a context for doing the assignment.
- The purpose of an IL assignment should be to help students become fluent not only in the research process but also in a chosen or assigned research topic.
- Assignments allow students to extend the learning gained through lectures, readings, and tutorials.
- Communicate your expectations for the assignment in the form of a rubric or criteria.
- Provide prompt grading and individualized feedback so that students have time to reflect on their performance and can incorporate their learning into subsequent assignments and tests.
- To prevent plagiarism, create assignments that have a number of parts that build on each other throughout the course.
- Do all the assignments yourself to discover issues with the assignment that you can correct beforehand.
- Collaborative group work in an online course offers a number of benefits for students and instructors.
- You can cut down on workload issues by providing students with readings on pre-assigned topics.
- Peer review work is a simple way to include collaborative group work elements into your course.

APPENDIX 1

Resource 7.1
Sample Assignments for Graduate Students

Assignment 1: Searching for Dissertations and Theses/Introduction to the Literature Review

ACRL Information Literacy Competency Standards

Standard Two, Outcome 2.3.a. Uses various search systems to retrieve information in a variety of formats.

Standard Four, Outcome 4.1.a. Organizes the content in a manner that supports the purposes and format of the product or performance.

Unit Learning Outcomes
By the end of this module, students will be able to:
- Identify databases that can be used to find dissertations and theses.
- Search effectively to locate both UA and non-UA dissertations and theses.
- Understand the different types of literature reviews.
- Know what is expected for a literature review in a graduate thesis or dissertation.
- Correctly cite a dissertation or thesis according to the chosen citation style guide.

Submission Instructions:
- Record your responses to the assignment in this Word document and upload to the D2L Dropbox.
- Name the Dropbox file in the following way: [your last name]Wk6Assgnmt.doc. example: NewbyWk6Assgnmt.doc
- Be sure and fill in your name below.
- This assignment is worth 25 points.
- Due date: Sunday, July 14, 11:59 PM.

Name:

Research Portfolio Alert! You are encouraged to add citations for relevant dissertations or theses to your Research Portfolio under the Annotated Bibliography section.

Introduction:
In this assignment, you will search the dissertation/theses databases that you were introduced to in this week's module to locate dissertations/theses in your focused research area. You are not required to export the records to your citation management tool (RefWorks or EndNote), but you may want to do that anyway. In the second part of this assignment, you will be asked to scan dissertation/theses for the literature review and comment on how this lit review differs from what you have learned in this module and what aspects would you like to adopt for your own dissertation/thesis lit review.

Part 1. Searching Non-UA Dissertations/Theses in the ProQuest Dissertations & Theses (PQDT) database (10 points)

  a. Search the research topic used in previous LIBR 696a modules in the ProQuest Dissertations & Theses (PQDT) database. List your search statement here (5 points):

  b. From your search results, select one thesis or dissertation from another university (non-UA). Provide the bibliographic citation for the dissertation/thesis in a standard citation format.
  (ProQuest has a Cite feature like EbscoHost's that will format the reference in the style of your choice. Be sure to double-check for accuracy.)
  (5 points)
  1. Citation style used (APA, Chicago, MLA, etc.):
  2. Citation:

Part 2. Searching the Dissertations & Theses @ University of Arizona database (15 points)
Note: You can also find UA dissertations & theses in the full PQDT database but we want you to have some experience & awareness of the @UA sub-set of PQDT.

a. Search Dissertations & Theses @ University of Arizona using your advisor's name or your department.

To do this:

- On the Advanced Search (default) page, on the far right side in the first row of the search box area change the field to be searched using the drop down menu.
  - Choose either "Advisor—ADV" or "Department—DEP" and search with your advisor's name or your department.
  - Alternatively, in the middle of the search page under "Search Options" use the Advisor search box. (There is not one for Department in this section.)

If your research topic does not correlate closely with your department or advisor, choose a likely corresponding department at the University of Arizona. For example, if you are studying international law that has to do with commerce, choose the Economics Dept. or another relevant department.

b. List the advisor's name or department searched (2 points):

c. From the results, choose a dissertation or thesis that is available full-text online and that is relevant (as possible) to your research topic. Provide the bibliographic citation for this publication. Use the citation style selected in Part 1 above. (See examples of citations for dissertations/theses in Part 2 of this week's module.) (3 points)

d. Retrieve the full-text of the dissertation/thesis and scan the literature review and bibliography.

Reflect in writing on the literature review and bibliography sections as they relate to the readings in Week 6, Part 2 (Literature Review). (10 points)

- How are they consistent and how they differ from the guidance in the readings?
- What features or approaches taken would you like to adopt for your own dissertation/theses literature review and bibliography?
- Provide your written response here:

Assignment 2: Social Media and Scholarly Networking

ACRL Information Literacy Competency Standards:

Standard 3, Performance Indicator 6: The information literate student validates understanding and interpretation of the information through discourse with other individuals, subject-area experts, and/or practitioners.

Unit Learning Outcomes
Students will be able to:
- Identify social networking and collaboration tools which are useful for scholarly/academic purposes.
- Describe the positive and negative implications of social media for scholarly networking.

Assigned Readings:
- Gruzd, Anatoliy, Kathleen Staves, and Amanda Wilk, "Connected Scholars: Examining the Role of Social Media in Research Practices of Faculty Using the UTAUT Model," *Computers in Human Behavior*, 28, no. 6:(2012): 2340–2350. doi:10.1016/j.chb.2012.07.004 (Focus on the Sections 1–5 and 8.)
- Mangan, Katherine, "Social Networks for Academics Proliferate, Despite Some Doubts," *The Chronicle of Higher Education*. (2012, April 29). http://chronicle.com/article/Social-Networks-for-Academics/131726/ (Read the article and the comments.)

Submission Instructions:
- Go to the Discussion folder for this week's assignment.
- This assignment is worth 25 points.
- Due date: Sunday, August 4, 11:59 PM.

Discussion Assignment

In this discussion assignment, you will need to have read the articles listed above to respond fully to the questions. Please comment in a thoughtful and substantive manner on the following items:
- What is your opinion about the value (positive and negative) of social media for scholarly/research networking? Refer to the readings and your own experiences. (15 points)
- Respond in a substantive way to the comments of at least one other student. (10 points)

APPENDIX 2

Resource 7.2
Sample Assignments for Undergraduate Students

Assignment 1: Comparing Sources—Guns Topic

Your name: _____

Your research question: Should people be allowed to carry guns on college campuses?

ACRL Information Literacy Competency Standards
Standard Three: The information literate student evaluates information and its sources critically and incorporates selected information into his or her knowledge base and value system.

Unit Learning Outcomes
Students will be able to:
- Differentiate between popular and scholarly sources
- Discuss different viewpoints related to your topic
- Identify bias in articles
- Identify the bibliographic information of different information sources

Total Points: 25

Directions: For this assignment you will use one of the library's most popular databases, Academic Search Complete, to access and read different types of articles. After you read both articles, answer the questions in the table on the following page.

Submission Instructions:
- Save file by clicking File > Save As
- Rename file with your last and first name (e.g., SmithJohnAssignment4)
- Save as type: Word Document
- Once you have saved the assignment, upload it to D2L Dropbox, Assignment 1

This assignment is due by June 17, 7:59 AM (Tucson time)

PART 1: Accessing the Articles

To access Academic Search Complete from the UA Library Homepage, click Search & Find > Articles & Databases > Academic Search Complete

Article 1

- In the keyword search box type in "how many more guns?" and click Search.
- Find the record for the article titled "How Many More Guns?: Estimating the Effect of Allowing Licensed Concealed Handguns on a College Campus" by Jeffrey A. Bouffard, et al.
- Click the link: Linked Full Text, to read the full article.

Article 2

- In Academic Search Complete, click Clear to begin a new search.
- In the keyword search box type in "When College Students Pack Heat" and click Search.
- Find the record for the article titled "When College Students Pack Heat, the Danger Grows."
- Click the link: PDF Full Text, to read the full article.

PART 2: Analyzing the Articles

Once you have read both articles, fill in the table with your answers.

	"How Many More Guns?: Estimating the Effect of Allowing Licensed Concealed Handguns on a College Campus" by Jeffrey A. Bouffard, et al.	*"When College Students Pack Heat, the Danger Grows"*
Author(s)		
Title of journal or periodical		
Date of publication		
Number of pages		
In your own words (no quoting!) provide a summary of the article.		
What is the purpose of the article?		

Who is the intended audience?		
Describe the language.		
What are the author's credentials?		
Describe the author's attitude toward the subject: • What kind of tone is used? • What biases, if any, do you detect?		
Evaluate the author's argument: • What sources are used to support his or her claims? • Do the sources seem credible? • Does the author make a clear distinction between opinions and facts?		
Does the author include citations (in-text and bibliography)?		
Describe the appearance: photos, graphs, tables, etc.		
What is the word count of the article? How many pages?		
Is this a scholarly or a popular source?		

Assignment 2—More Research Options

Your name:

Your research question:

ACRL Information Literacy Competency Standards
Standard Two: The information literate student accesses needed information effectively and efficiently.

Unit Learning Outcomes

- Create effective search strings
- Describe Academic Search Complete
- Use Academic Search Complete to locate sources
- Locate and use e-books in the library catalog
- Use the UA library catalog to locate different sources

Total points: 25

Submission Instructions:
- Save file by clicking File > Save As
- Rename file with your last and first name (e.g., SmithJohnAssignment6)
- Save as type: Word Document
- Once you have saved the assignment, upload it to D2L Dropbox, Assignment 3
        This assignment is due by July 15, 7:59 AM (Tucson time)

Part A: Using the Library Catalog

1. Julian is writing a research paper about gay marriage debates in the United States and needs to find books in the library on this subject. He needs to make sure the books are current (published no later than 2002) and scholarly (meaning it includes bibliographic references and was written by someone with an advanced degree in the field).

   a. If Julian wants to conduct a phrase search, should he enter gay marriage or "gay marriage" in the search box? Why does it make a difference if he uses quotation marks or not?

b. The UA library catalog uses Library of Congress subject headings to identify all of the books or articles that deal with a particular topic. Julian wants to find out if gay marriage is a subject heading. Is it? How did you search the catalog to find this answer?

2. Find the catalog record for this book and then answer the questions below.

Title: *Same-Sex Marriage*
Author: Allene Phy-Olsen
Publication date: 2006
ISBN: 0313335168

a. What is the call number of this book?

b. What floor of the Main Library is this book located on? (Please explain how you found this information.)

3. Julian has found two additional book records that look promising: (This question requires you to do a little independent research.)

	Book 1	Book 2
Title	*Does Legalizing Same-Sex Marriage Really Harm Individuals, Families, or Society?*	*Why Marriage?: The History Shaping Today's Debate over Gay Equality*
Author/Editor	Lynn D. Wardle	George Chauncey
Publication date	2008	2004
ISBN	0761843167	0465009573

Before Julian makes a trip to the library, he wants to find out a little bit more about the authors. The catalog record does not give him much information about the authors' credentials or politics. What can you find out about these authors—are they qualified to write about the gay marriage debate? Would you feel comfortable citing them in an academic paper? Why or why not?

Part B. Finding E-books

Use the UA library catalog to find an e-book on your research topic. The book should be scholarly (i.e., published by a university scholarly press and it should include bibliographical references).

1. Once you've found the book, use the catalog's detailed record to fill out the following information.

   a. Author:
   b. Title:
   c. Call Number:
   d. Publisher:
   e. Subjects:
   f. Year of Publication:

2. Write a paragraph (5 to 10 sentences) about your experience using the UA library catalog to find an e-book. What was your search strategy? Did you use keywords, phrases, subject headings? Did you have to try more than one search?

3. Provide a summary of the book and how you can use it in your research. This will require you to look at the first few pages, the TOC, the introduction, and to skim through it.

4. Have you used an e-book before, or searched for one through the library catalog? Which format do you prefer, and why?

PART C: Using Academic Search Complete

Use Academic Search Complete (ASC) to locate one SCHOLARLY source related to your topic. Then, write the citation in MLA format below. You will miss points if your source is not scholarly, or if you do not use MLA appropriately.

1. Write a citation for the article you found in correct MLA format:

2. Write a paragraph (5 to 10 sentences) about your experience using Academic Search Complete to find an article. In your paragraph address the following:
   - Is this your first time using ASC?
   - What did you think of it?
   - Will you use it in the future for other courses?
   - What was your search strategy?
   - Did you use keywords, phrases, subject headings?
   - Did you have to try more than one search?

NOTES

1. Barbara Fister, "Welcome to the Palace of Ambiguity," *Library Babel Fish* (blog), *Inside Higher Ed,* July 18, 2013, available at http://www.insidehighered.com/blogs/library-babel-fish/welcome-palace-ambiguity#ixzz2bJFrc100, accessed January 16, 2014.

2. Barbara Fister, "Welcome to the Palace of Ambiguity"; Wendy Holliday and Jim Rogers, "Talking about Information Literacy: The Mediating Role of Discourse in a College Writing Classroom," *portal: Libraries and the Academy,* 13, no. 3 (2013): 257–271. http://muse.jhu.edu/.

3. "Defining Critical Thinking," *Foundation for Critical Thinking,* 2013, available at http://www.criticalthinking.org/pages/defining-critical-thinking/766, accessed January 16, 2014.

4. Joanna M. Burkhardt and Mary C. MacDonald, with Andrée J. Rathemacher, *Teaching Information Literacy: 50 Standards-based Exercises for College Students,* 2nd ed. (Chicago: American Library Association, 2010).

5. Celeste Fenton and Brenda Ward Watkins, *Fluency in Distance Learning* (Charlotte, NC: Information Age Publishing, Inc., 2010), 90.

6. Rena M. Palloff and Keith Pratt, *The Virtual Student: a Profile and Guide to Working with Online Learners* (San Francisco: Jossey-Bass, 2003), 35.

7. L. W. Anderson and, and D. R. Krathwohl, ed., *A Taxonomy for Learning, Teaching, and Assessing: A Revision of Bloom's Taxonomy of Educational Objectives* (New York, London: Addison Wesley, Longmann, 2001).

8. Joan R. Kaplowitz, *Transforming Information Literacy Instruction Using Learner-Centered Teaching* (New York: Neal-Shulman Publishers, 2012), 104.

9. Kaplowitz, *Transforming Information Literacy,* 104.

10. E.C. Boling et al., "Cutting the Distance in Distance Education: Perspectives on What Promotes Positive, Online Learning Experiences," *Internet and Higher Education,* (2012), 121.

11. Patricia Deubel. "Learning from Reflections-Issues in Building Quality Online Courses," *Online Journal of Distance Learning Administration,* 6, no. 3 (2003), available at http://www.westga.edu/~distance/ojdla/fall63/deubel63.htm, accessed January 16, 2014.

12. Barbara Gross Davis, *Tools for Teaching* (San Francisco: Jossey-Bass, 1993), 234.

13. Davis. *Tools for Teaching*, 233.

14. L. B. Samuels and C. M. Bast. "Strategies to Help Legal Studies Students Avoid Plagiarism," *Journal of Legal Studies Education,* 23 (2006), 151–167. doi: 10.1111/j.1744-1722.2006.00026.x.

15. James E. Kasprzak and Mary Anne Nixon, "Cheating in Cyberspace: Maintaining Quality in Online Education," *AACE Journal* 12, no. 1 (2004), 85–99.

16. A. Reed and T. Perfetti, "Dealing with Online Cheating and Plagiarism in Adult Education," In *Proceedings of World Conference on E-Learning in Corporate, Government, Healthcare, and Higher Education*, edited by T. Bastiaens and G. Marks (Chesapeake, VA: AACE, 2012), 1252.

17. Debra Humphreys, "Deploying Collaborative Leadership to Reinvent Higher Education for the Twenty-First Century," *Peer Review* 15, no. 1 (Winter 2013), available at http://www.aacu.org/peerreview/pr-wi13/Humphreys.cfm, accessed January 16, 2014.

18. Carnegie Mellon University. Eberly Center, "What Are the Benefits of Group Work?" *Teaching Excellence & Educational Innovation*, available at http://www.cmu.edu/teaching/designteach/design/instructionalstrategies/groupprojects/benefits.html, accessed January 16, 2014.

19. Worcester Polytechnic Institute. "Tips for Participating in Group Work Online," available at http://www.wpi.edu/Academics/ATC/Collaboratory/Teaching/onlinegrouptips.pdf, accessed January 16, 2014.

20. Kaplowitz, *Transforming Information Literacy Instruction*, 79.

21. Ibid., 78.

22. Ray Martinez, April, Shen-Yi Cheng, Kennon Smith, Matt Smith, and Sangil Yoon, "Indiana University Instructional Systems Technology (IST) Graduate Student Attitudes towards Group Work," *Indiana University*, available at http://www.indiana.edu/~educy520/sec5982/week_15/rmacksmssy.pdf, accessed January 16, 2014

23. Susan Ko and Steve Rossen, *Teaching Online: A Practical Guide*, 2nd. (New York: Routledge, 2008), 122.

24. Ibid., 203.

25. Ibid., 202.

Chapter Eight

But Did They Learn Anything?
Assessing and Evaluating

"Educators do not teach and then assess; nor do they think of assessment as something that is done to students. Instead, they consider the assessment activity itself the instructional episode."

—Judith A. Arter[1]

INTRODUCTION

We often view assessment as coming at the end of the learning activity, but by that time, both students and instructors are fatigued and just want to get it over with. We may think "assessment is hard," and that we are not familiar with assessments that require statistical analysis. Often we do not have the time to create and grade complex assessments that measure student performance. Most importantly, perhaps we may wonder if the assessment is really measuring learning. If you have these concerns, read on.

Assessment is an integral part of the learning process and like other aspects of teaching and learning, it requires time and practice. Learning assessments show students what they understand and are capable of doing, as well as areas that need improvement. As will be shown later in this chapter, an assessment can be the learning activity itself, so that students are learning and being assessed simultaneously. For instructors, assessments identify areas where students are having difficulties, and by analyzing assessment results, instructors can make informed decisions on where the course can be improved. For academic institutions, assessments provide measures of student accomplishment and academic program performance. This evidence demonstrates to external organizations and the public that academic institutions are effective in providing quality education.

Although learning assessments concern gathering evidence of student understanding and performance, there is more to assessment than counting up the correct number of points and assigning a grade at the end of the semester. In this chapter we begin with the assessment cycle, a framework for assessment design that leads to better student learning outcomes and course improvements. We explain two learning assessment concepts, formative and summative assessment, giving examples of each and how they are used in the learning process. Most of the chapter focuses on examples of objective and performance assessments, along with techniques for creating effective multiple-choice test questions and rubrics to measure performance levels. Evaluation of teaching effectiveness will also be addressed, as well as ideas on how to prevent cheating in an online environment.

THE ASSESSMENT CYCLE

The assessment cycle is a continuous, cyclical process with the goal of improving student learning and revising the course to enhance the learning experience. Gilchrist and Zald's assessment design model uses a set of questions to represent key elements of the assessment cycle.[2] The remainder of this chapter will focus on how best to address these design questions:

- What do we want students to achieve?
- How will we know students have met the outcomes?
- How will the students demonstrate their learning and ability?
- What did we learn from the assessment?
- What course improvements need to be made as a result of our assessment data?

FORMATIVE AND SUMMATIVE ASSESSMENT

Assessment of student learning is often characterized as either formative (developmental) or summative (cumulative/evaluative). Although the same assessment methods can be used for both, as their names imply, the assessments are used for very different purposes.[3]

Formative assessments are used to provide students with feedback on the strengths and weaknesses in their understanding or performance. For example, in our online graduate student course, we use weekly assignments as formative assessments to provide feedback students can use to improve their performance in subsequent assignments. This assessment approach is also referred to as *assessment for learning* because the assessment not only measures what the student is able to do, but also serves as the instructional activity.[4] An interactive tutorial that directs students to perform a task and then provides instant feedback on their performance is another example of an assessment for learning activity.

Summative assessments, such as evaluations of a final course project, paper, presentation, or standardized test are used to provide evidence of cumulative learning, usually to the academic institution, for accountability purposes. Summative assessments can also be used to demonstrate the value added by instruction, such as the value of programmatic IL instruction that can be correlated with students' future academic success.[5] Summative assessments are not intended as a learning activity. However, they are integral to the learning process. For better or worse, summative assessments that result in grades are a motivating force for students because students want good grades to obtain or maintain scholarships, to be admitted to quality graduate schools, to please their parents, and as a reward for their learning accomplishments.

ASSESSMENT METHODS

In the assessment design process, assessment methods answer the questions: (1) how will students demonstrate their ability and understanding? and (2) what evidence will we gather? Our exploration of these questions will focus on objective and performance-based methods.

Objective Assessment

Objective assessment measures students' knowledge or understanding using fixed-choice questions, such as multiple-choice, matching, or true or false. Students are familiar with this type of assessment method, and it can be used to assess understanding of a greater amount of content than performance-based assessments.[6] One of the biggest advantages of using objective assessments are that they are easy and time saving to administer and score, especially using the LMS quiz function. Furthermore, objective assessments can be highly reliable and "tend to have a higher predictive validity with GPA and standardized test scores."[7] However, valid and reliable questions are not easy to create. They require expertise in writing good fixed-choice questions and repeated large scale testing and statistical analysis to identify questions that need to be revised or deleted.

In our online graduate and undergraduate courses we administer pre- and post-tests made up primarily of multiple-choice and short answer questions.

(See Resource 8.1 Pre- and Post-Test Questions). Students complete the pre-test in the first week of the course and we use the results to learn about students' experiences conducting library research and their understanding of information literacy concepts. In the post-test, we ask the same information literacy questions as in the pre-test to measure student learning gains. In the graduate course, we also ask students to self-assess their ability to conduct library research and use citation management software both in the pre- and post-test as another indicator of improved performance in each of these key areas of our course.

In our instruction team's annual report to the library, we use the results of undergraduate course post-tests to demonstrate that we have met our instruction quality standards:

- 90 percent of the students who complete the Research Lab course successfully demonstrate a baseline of information literacy competence (70 percent or better on post-test).
- Students will have an average 20-percent increase between their pre and post-test scores.

We have met this quality standard each year that we have taught the course. We also report on students' final grades.

Although used solely within the course, our pre- and post-testing has allowed us to demonstrate to the library and the university administration the value of our online courses. We conducted a research study to compare student learning in the undergraduate online IL course with other methods, including one-shot sessions taught by librarians and English graduate teaching assistants. After administering pre- and post-tests to students in a first-year composition course, we used statistical analysis to show that students do not start the course with IL skills and abilities. We were also able to show that students who completed our undergraduate online course had gained more IL competency than those students who had a different IL instructional experience.[8] We used these results to convince the campus administration that an online IL course was valuable to students, and we were awarded funding for graduate teaching assistants to help teach several sections of the course.

Developing Good Multiple-Choice Items

Multiple-choice tests are one of the most popular types of objective fixed-item assessments. They are often perceived as being limited in their ability to assess learning outcomes beyond the knowledge and comprehension levels. However, higher-order thinking skills such as application and evaluation can be assessed when the multiple-choice item is presented to the student in a new

Table 8.1.   Multiple-Choice Test Items Aligned with Bloom's Taxonomy

Knowledge	What are three characteristics of scholarly sources?
Comprehension	What will happen when an * is added to the end of a word?
Application	You are searching the effects of a low-carbohydrate diet on college-age women. Which search string would work best if you were conducting a Boolean search in Academic Search Complete?
Analysis and Evaluation	You are researching how architects are using neuroscience research to design better health-care facilities. You need to locate current primary research articles that have been published in academic journals. Access the three articles by clicking on the hyperlinks. Then answer this question: Which article would work best for this particular research need?

context.[9] Table 8.1 gives examples of different multiple-choice test items aligned with Bloom's Taxonomy (see chapter 3 for more information on Bloom's Taxonomy). Note that we do not recommend fixed-choice items for outcomes measuring synthesis.

Writing multiple-choice items is easy but writing good ones takes time and practice.[10] Here we offer some basic tips for constructing better multiple-choice items. Many of these tips are adapted from Linn and Gronlund.[11]

First, you should familiarize yourself with the basic terminology used in a multiple-choice test item construction:

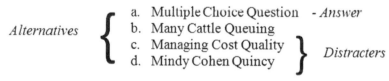

Figure 8.1.   Multiple Choice Test Item Terminology

Explanation of Terms

Stem: The prompt that indicates what the student needs to do. Most often written as a question but can also be written as a complete statement. For this reason, we use the term *multiple-choice item* and not *question*.

Alternatives: All of the options students can choose from.

Distractors: Alternatives that are incorrect. They are meant to distract the student from the correct answer.

Answer: The correct alternative.

One of the most common mistakes you can make when creating multiple-choice items is unknowingly helping students eliminate distractors by creating ones that do not quite fit with the rest of the item components in some way. This example illustrates the use of poor alternatives:

1. From this screen, how should you proceed to request a book from another library?
   a. click Interlibrary Loan
   b. go to the Services page
   c. access your account
   d. when you receive an e-mail from the City Director for Public Relations office in your campus inbox

Distractor D in this example illustrates several problems with poorly written alternatives. First, it looks different than the others because it is much longer. It is also syntactically different than the other alternatives, and it does not fit grammatically with the stem because the stem is clearly asking for an action. In addition to looking and acting differently, D is also different in its content. All of the other alternatives except D are plausible options that refer to terms the students should be familiar with from the course content. However, students will most likely not have encountered the office referred to in option D.

Another problem with this item is the use of the word *library* in both the stem and in the answer. Use of the same word in both the stem and the answer should be avoided so as not to give away the answer to the student. Of course, you may want to throw students off by including the same word in a distractor. With this example in mind we offer the following guidelines when creating alternatives for multiple-choice items:

1. Make all alternatives of approximately the same length
2. Make all alternatives syntactically similar
3. Make all alternatives grammatically correct with the stem
4. Make all alternatives plausible
5. Make all alternatives on the same subject matter
6. Make all alternatives based on course content that is familiar to students
7. Do not include key words in the answer that also occur in the stem

Both stems and alternatives should not be confusing to the student and should be kept as simple as possible. After all, you are not testing how well the student can read a purposefully complicated or tricky question, but rather how well they have achieved a learning outcome. Stems can be written as questions or as incomplete statements; choose the one that is easiest to understand. With simplicity and ease of understanding as guiding principles, we offer the following tips and examples as a starting point:

1. Do not include irrelevant information in the stem that is not needed for the student to understand what he or she must do. Note the differences in the two examples given here. The first option includes unnecessary information that is not needed to understand the question.
    - University students enjoy the use of the library twenty-four hours a day most of the school year. If you wanted to find out the library hours during Spring Break, where on the library web site would you need to look?
    - Library hours can be found under which area of the web page?
2. Although the stem should remain as simple and readable as possible, you do not want to include too little information. This can cause your alternatives to be lengthy and repetitive, and you do not want students spending their time reading long alternatives instead of answering questions. In the first example, the alternatives contain information that could be supplied in the stem. The second example shows the information in the stem instead of repeatedly in the alternatives.
    - What is the information cycle?
        a. It is a theory about how information can be easily deleted and essentially killed by anyone with access to the web.
        b. It is the process and progression by which information is created in different formats after an event occurs.
        c. It is an explanation for why people with better socioeconomic means have better access to information throughout their lives.
        d. It is a cloud-based tool that allows someone to easily recycle information for future use.
    - The information cycle explains how information _____.
        a. is digitized for greater use
        b. can be sent over the web
        c. is created over a period of time
        d. transfers from one format to another
3. The stem should contain sufficient information for the students to readily understand what is required of them. In the first example, it is not clear what the problem is or what information the student must supply. This is cleared up in the second example.
    - The main library _____.
    - Where is the main library located?
4. Many times an item may not have one absolute correct answer as is often the case when selecting one information source over another. When there is no definite correct answer, use *best* or *most* as in the example below.

- Which database can you use to locate scholarly articles?
- Which database would work best in helping you to locate scholarly articles?

5. Do not use *not* or other negative statements. *Not* can be confusing, and it can be easily overlooked even when it is bolded and capitalized. Linn and Gronlund recommend using negative statements only in dire, life or death-type situations such as a nurse choosing the wrong drug to administer or a pilot choosing the wrong course of action.[12]

6. Similar to the use of negative statements, using *none of the above, all of the above*, and *choose two* can be confusing for students especially when they have been working on items thus far that did not ask for two answers. Additionally, as Linn and Gronlund point out, these types of items can lead to students just eliminating the distractors without ever testing to see if the student actually knows the correct answer.[13]

7. Your goal in creating a multiple-choice test is to get an accurate as possible assessment of student's achievement of the course learning outcomes. As such, you want to avoid cognitive overload as much as possible. Using tricky or complicated questions and switching the type of items you are asking from multiple-choice to true or false to matching will force the student to spend time figuring out what he or she is supposed to do instead of concentrating on the content of the item.

8. Include as many alternatives as is needed for the item. For some items, three may be enough, whereas others may require more. Keep in mind that students will be able to guess much easier when there are fewer alternatives.

9. Avoid culturally sensitive topics or topics that may bring up negative associations. Similar to avoiding overloading students' cognitively, you also want to avoid negatively impacting them affectively, or emotionally. This, of course, would be impossible if you were teaching a course on a topic such as the Holocaust. However, in an information literacy course, you can avoid the types of issues that are potentially more sensitive.

Objective Assessment Tools

Multiple-choice quizzes and tests are easy to set up using the LMS quiz module. You can quickly create question items, or import items from the LMS question library or from a previous quiz used externally to the LMS. You can also easily specify start and end dates, designate the amount of time allowed to take the test, the number of attempts, and special access for students with disabilities. Also, you will be able to randomize the order of a set of questions and the order of alternative answers within a question. You can create statistical reports that display score distribution, question difficulty levels, and the class average, among others. An analysis of the statistical reports will help identify where students are struggling, as well as which question items need to be revised.

In addition to the LMS quiz module and the question library, there are also commercial testing and survey products that are Question & Test Interoperability (QTI) compliant, which means that question items can be seamlessly imported into the LMS. We store our question items in Respondus, an assessment authoring tool that is compliant with many LMS products. Respondus gives us the flexibility to export question items, not only to the LMS but also to create online quizzes for research studies and usability testing.

In our exploration of commercial survey and testing products, we found that many have costly licensing fees and are targeted for large departments or programs, such as a business or marketing program. We have not identified any testing or survey programs that had the capacity to add metadata, such as ACRL IL Standards annotations. Another consideration is whether or not the commercial product has the capability to import scores to the LMS grade book. When we use Survey Monkey for our mid-course evaluation, we have to manually input the five points we award for the survey into the grade book. In addition, we have to keep track of who has completed the survey.

Performance Assessment

Performance assessment, also referred to as authentic assessment, involves students actively applying what they have learned in a real-world context.[14] This assessment method offers opportunities to design assessments that are complex and open-ended and that can measure higher-level thinking skills, such as analyzing, evaluating, and synthesizing information.[15] Examples of performance assessments include case studies or problem-based assignments, as well as research papers, portfolios, and presentations. According to Kaplowitz, "Research has shown that learners are more attentive and motivated if the material being taught has some connection to their real life. The more our assessments seem to mimic real-world situations, the more integral they come to learning itself."[16]

In our online graduate course, we have a number of assignments that can be described as performance or authentic assessments. In one of our units, we ask students to conduct a cited reference search in the *Web of Science* database using an influential publication or major author in their field to locate related publications that may be useful for their own research. In this assessment, students are asked to apply their searching knowledge and abilities in a slightly different manner than a typical database search to locate the citing references. They can use this ability throughout their research careers, especially when moving into a new area of research where they are not familiar with the major researchers.

Another example from our graduate course is the research portfolio, which provides cumulative evidence of what the student has learned and accomplished throughout the course. It directly reflects our course learning outcomes:

Students will be able to:

- Demonstrate their knowledge and use of information sources
- Successfully create and apply search strategies
- Apply ethical and legal standards in their information use
- Effectively manage citations using citation management software

At the beginning of the course, we provide a detailed list of requirements for the research portfolio which are used as criteria for assessing the portfolio. (See Resource 8.2 Research Portfolio Requirements) Students create their research portfolios using Google Sites, Weebly, or other web authoring programs.

Performance assessments, when designed well, offer a wealth of information about what a student is able to do in a much more granular way than an objective assessment. However, not every assessment should be performance based. An effective performance assessment can take a great deal of time to develop because you must create an appropriate task and criteria or rubrics to measure student performance, as well as time to review, grade, and provide feedback. It will also take students more time to provide evidence of their learning than an objective assessment.[17] When using performance assessments, remember to include sufficient time in the course schedule for students to complete the assessment and for you to grade and provide feedback.

Rubrics

It is often the case that performance assessments, being more complex, are more difficult to assess objectively. This is where rubrics can be used to define performance levels in a precise manner. Rubrics can be defined as a set of standards or guidelines that describe levels of performance with an associated point scale.[18] For instructors, a rubric makes it easier to assess student work and to be more consistent in the scoring process.

There are two basic types of rubrics: analytic and holistic. Wiggins and McTighe describe analytic rubrics as "evaluating each student's product or performance on more than one dimension."[19] Holistic rubrics describe and score an entire product or performance as a whole. Whereas analytic rubrics take more time to create than holistic rubrics, analytic rubrics provide more

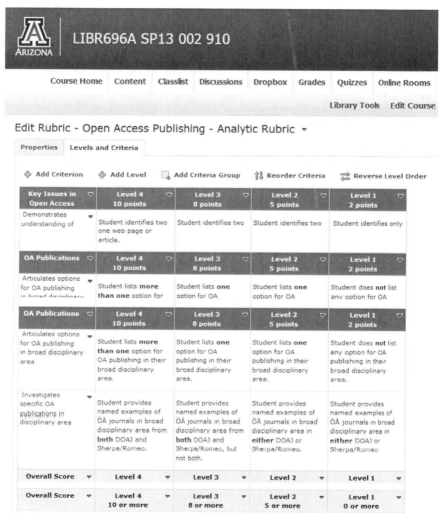

Figure 8.2.   Analytic Rubric—Open Access Publishing Assignment

detailed feedback to both the student and instructor about what a student understands or is able to do. Figure 8.2 shows an analytic rubric using the D2L rubric tool in our graduate course. Figure 8.3 shows a holistic rubric for the Research Portfolio assignment.

Making rubrics available to students raises the bar on learning and performance. Research studies show that students perform better when they are aware of the rubrics that will be used to assess their performance.[20] Another advantage in using rubrics is that it can reduce student frustration or confusion about how an assessment was scored.[21] Wiggins and McTighe suggest

Level	Start Range	Description	Feedback
Excellent ▾	90 % or more	Meets or exceeds all the requirements for the research portfolio.	
Good ▾	80 % or more	Meets many of the requirements, but is incomplete in one category, excluding the annotated bibliography.	
Satisfactory ▾	70 % or more	Some components of the research portfolio are missing or incomplete. The annotated bibliography is correct and complete.	
▾ Unsatisfactory	0 % or more	More than two areas of the requirements are missing or incomplete. The annotated bibliography is missing or incomplete.	

Figure 8.3.   Holistic Rubric—Research Portfolio Assignment

providing students with multiple examples of what each performance level in a rubric looks like.[22] These examples can also be useful if more than one instructor is involved in using the rubric.

Although there are a number of advantages in using rubrics, according to Oakleaf, "crafting a good rubric requires time, practice and revision."[23] As a starting point, we offer the following brief overview on writing rubrics adapted from Oakleaf, and Wiggins and McTighe.[24]

1. Determine the most significant learning outcomes you want to measure. The assessment should directly reflect the learning outcomes.
2. Gather evidence and develop evaluative criteria.
   a. Identify examples of outstanding student performance/work for a specific aspect or criterion and determine the attributes that exemplify this aspect.
   b. Find examples of student work that demonstrates low performance for a specific aspect or criterion. Describe the characteristics of these works in terms of the learning outcomes. You now have clearly defined criteria for both high and low ends of the performance scale.
   c. The next task is to identify and examine student work that falls into the middle category and develop evaluative criterion for this level.
3. Determine the number of performance levels you will use in the rubric. This will depend largely on the range of student performance in the class. You may wish to more finely distinguish between performance levels, such as below average and above average.
4. Write descriptions for each performance level.
   • Find the middle ground between over-generalizing and being too specific.[25] Generalizations will make it difficult to distinguish one performance level from another. If the descriptions are too specific, there is little flexibility for variation within a performance level.

- Focus on how well students can accomplish the task, not how many times they can do it.
- Use parallel language for all performance level descriptions to increase clarity for both the student and the instructor.
- Avoid library jargon that will not be understood by students or teaching assistants who may be using the rubric.
- Don't use overly negative language for low performance. Oakleaf reminds us: "Performance level labels should be descriptive, not discouraging."[26]

5. Revise the rubric. Wiggins and McTighe recommend revising the rubric after each use to improve the clarity and precision of the rubric.[27]

If more than one instructor is using the same set of assessments and rubrics, then it is advisable for everyone to participate in a rubrics norming session. In the session instructors can learn details about the underlying context and content of the rubric, clarify the meaning of each performance level, and practice using the rubric so that everyone rates student performance with a similar score.[28]

A rubrics template tool should be available in your LMS. The rubrics template provides options for the number of performance levels and the scoring range, as well as space to write evaluative criterion for each performance level. Once you set up the rubric it will be much faster to review and score the assessment.

If you do not have the time to create your own rubrics, there are numerous examples of quality rubrics for information literacy topics in the education and library literature.[29]

Student Performance Reports within the LMS

It is well worth exploring the wealth of student activity data that you can glean from your LMS and that can be used in assigning grades for participation in the course. For example, in Desire2Learn there is a Student Progress Tool, that displays performance indicators for each student in areas such as content completion (topics visited); login history; discussion participation summary; grade information for each assignment; and quiz participation. For a perspective on how much time on task was spent by a specific student, you can view reports that show the number of visits to content topic page and how long the student spent on the page. The Dropbox/Assignment module also provides information about when students submitted their assignments (usually on the due date), the date that the assignment was scored, and whether or not students read the feedback, if provided.

Peer Assessment

Peer assessment is "an interactive process of review, assessment and feedback to fellow students for the purpose of enhancing their own and their peers' learning and achievement."[30] As mentioned in chapter 7, in our graduate course we have students evaluate each other's draft research portfolios. We decided to use this approach after we scored and provided feedback on the draft portfolio but did not see much in the way of improvement in the final portfolios. The peer evaluation led to more uniform and complete research portfolios. The peer evaluation was an opportunity for students to see what other portfolios looked like and gave them motivation to complete their own portfolio. Also, students enjoyed the peer assessment activity because it involved interacting with other students and offered them a different perspective on their portfolios.

It is worthwhile to take the time to help students understand the performance expectations and criteria for the peer assessment, whether it is for individual or group work. Alternatively, groups can develop their own set of criteria at the outset of a complex assignment. It is also useful to provide examples of appropriate and inappropriate feedback as part of the assignment and assessment process.[31]

Self-Assessment

Self-assessment gives students an opportunity to reflect on their learning and helps students to become better learners.[32] In our graduate course, we assign an end-of-course self-reflection in which students assess their learning/performance achievements in relation to the course learning outcomes. Students write about what they have learned and are able to do as a result of the course, and how it will help them as practitioners and researchers. From the self-assessment activity, we learn which course components are most effective in promoting learning.

A WORD ABOUT CHEATING

Preventing cheating in an online environment has its unique challenges. It also presents opportunities for designing assessments that make cheating much more difficult or not worth the effort. The following techniques represent best practices for creating assessments to avoid cheating. Many of the ideas mirror best practices for instructional design.

1. Conduct frequent assessments using a variety of assessment methods. Frequent and varied assessments will provide you with samples of stu-

dent work, so if there are discrepancies, it may indicate that cheating is occurring.[33]

2. Assign a low number of points for each assessment so that students are not tempted to cheat when the stakes are low.[34]

3. Avoid letting students select broad general topics that can be found in papers available on the Internet. Select a specific set of controversial topics that students can choose from. Davis advises that selecting topics "that are too difficult invites cheating, as do boring, trivial and uninteresting topics."[35]

4. Change the theme or topic for assignments and papers each time the course is offered.[36] Although it is time consuming to develop new topics, it prevents students from using graded assignments or papers from previous courses.

5. Use the LMS quiz module to randomize the order of the text questions and to randomize the order of the alternative answers for each question.[37]

6. Set up the quiz/test within the LMS so that the students will only be able to view test results not individual questions and answers.

7. Display one question at a time to discourage students from copying and pasting the questions and printing the entire test to give out to others.[38]

8. Develop a large question bank of reliable and valid questions so that you are able to offer versions of the test that have similar difficulty levels to students in the same class.[39]

9. If there are indications that cheating has occurred, use the LMS student progress tool to correlate dates of quiz completion with log-in dates and IP addresses.

10. Provide a clear statement in the syllabus that collaborating on assignments and quizzes and tests is not allowed.[40] We use this wording in our syllabus:

> Students are encouraged to share intellectual views and discuss freely the principles and applications of course materials. However, graded work/ exercises must be the product of independent effort unless otherwise instructed.

EVALUATING TEACHING EFFECTIVENESS

Throughout this chapter, we have presented learning assessment as not only focused on student achievement but also as an opportunity for improving the learning experience. In a similar fashion, evaluating teaching effectiveness is used to make summary judgments about the quality of the instruction and the course, as well as to provide information for teaching and course improvements. The following section describes commonly used methods for evaluating teaching effectiveness. We recommend using a variety of methods for a more valid and holistic picture about what worked in the course and what needs improvement.

Evidence from Student Learning Assessments

Although most of this chapter has focused on student learning assessment, it may seem redundant to mention it here, but using pre- and post-tests to measure gains in learning is a simple, yet effective way of measuring teaching quality. One of the issues to watch out for with pre- and post-testing is to ensure that the question items have been shown to effectively measure what they are intended to measure (validity) and that they have a high degree of consistency across tests (reliability). Another issue is the characteristics of a specific class that may be made up of students with low technology skills or other attributes that need to be taken into consideration when measuring gains in learning.

Teacher Course Evaluations

The Teacher Course Evaluation (TCE) is a standard evaluation practice mandated at most colleges and universities. TCEs have proved to be a reliable and valid measure of teaching effectiveness.[41] In many cases, TCEs are the only summative assessment of teacher/course effectiveness used by an institution. TCE ratings are included in annual faculty performance appraisals, in the tenure and promotion review process, for academic program evaluation, and teacher awards. Students also use TCE summary reports to select courses.[42]

TCE questions will vary from one institution to another, but are similar in scope. At our institution, students are asked to rate the overall instructor's teaching effectiveness compared to other instructors; the amount learned compared to other courses; and value of time spent on the course. Students can also enter free-form comments that provide more specific information than the rating scores. However, use caution in making course changes based on one or two student comments. Rather, make decisions by gathering comments over several semesters and looking for themes that indicate where course changes need to be made.

If you are implementing a credit course for the first time, you will need to be aware of the deadline for requesting the TCE service. There are options to add supplemental questions, such as questions that are applicable to online courses. Be aware that the return rate for TCEs in online courses is low. You will want to send out e-mails and post a news announcement reminding students to access and fill out the TCEs.

Student Surveys

Student surveys can also be used to gain insights into the effectiveness of specific aspects of the course. Because not all students complete the TCE form, a mandated student survey adds more information about where students are struggling and what is working well in the course. Here is a sampling of questions we ask in a mid-course survey in our graduate course:

1. Given that the LIBR 696a course was designed for "class" time + home-work time equivalent to the required hours for a one credit course (average 4 hours/week), do you see the actual workload as: (a) too much time (much more than 4 hours per week); (b) just right; (c) not enough time
2. What topic(s) would you like to spend more time on or see added to this course?
3. How do you see the instructor-student communication working for you? Please be specific and provide suggestions for improvements.
4. What comments or questions do you have about the D2L course site?

In our undergraduate course, we offer students extra-credit points for completing a short survey in which students are asked only two questions: (1) What did you enjoy the most about the course? (2) What would you like to change? For students to remain anonymous, they send their answers to an administrative assistant who compiles the feedback without names and then sends the list of names to the instructor so she can assign extra-credit points.

Self-Assessment

A good instructor knows that things can always be improved. One of the best methods of evaluating a course is through a self-evaluation of your own teaching. Take the time at the end of the course to reflect on what worked well and not so well. For a more formal approach, include a brief description of characteristics of students that were in the course, what difficulties they had, learning outcomes that were achieved, learning outcomes that were not met, and a reflection on possible reasons they were not met.[43] Although this exercise takes time, it provides a record of the state of the course for each semester and what needed improvement.

Peer Review

Peer evaluation can be an illuminating method for gaining insights into the strengths and weaknesses of your course. We have had colleagues co-teach our courses for a semester and this has given us a fresh perspective after teaching the same course for several semesters. Another resource for feedback on specific aspects of your course are staff from your campus teaching and learning center.

The Quality Matters (QM) peer evaluation process is also an option for peer review, previously mentioned in chapter 2. The QM standards rubrics for higher education are available on the QM web site, but you must first set up an account to view the rubrics document.[44] The QM standards are worth considering using either informally or formally because they are based on best practices in course design and online learning. The QM web site provides a list of current members, which may include your institution or local consortia. Although the QM peer review process is geared toward online courses that have been taught several times, the rubrics can be applied at any stage of the course development.

KNOW THIS . . .

- The assessment cycle provides a framework for viewing assessment as a cyclical process for continual improvement in learning and teaching.
- Use a variety of assessment methods to provide a more holistic picture of student learning and performance.
- Formative assessments help students become aware of the strengths and weaknesses of their performance.
- Summative assessments provide evidence of cumulative learning, usually to the academic institution for accountability purposes.
- Objective assessments are easy to administer and score. However, valid and reliable questions are not easy to create.
- Performance assessment involves students actively applying what they have learned in a real-world context.
- Researchers have found that students perform better when they are aware of the rubrics that will be used to assess their performance.
- Evaluation involves judging the effectiveness or quality of the instruction, at the individual teacher, course, or educational program level.
- Reflection and self-evaluation should be a routine part of every course you teach.

APPENDIX 1

Resource 8.1
Pre- and Post-Test Questions

1. How would you rate your ability to find appropriate information on a topic? Enter one of the following terms in the box below:

   Excellent, Good, Satisfactory, Generally Poor

2. How would you rate your ability to manage the information sources you use (e.g., keeping records of sources used)? Enter one of the following terms in the box below:

   Excellent, Good, Satisfactory, Generally Poor

3. For your research paper, you are considering researching the diet of women in Nordic countries such as Denmark. Choose the search statement that would get the best results.

   Question options:
   a. diets and women and Nord* and Denmark and (female not male)
   b. female diets and Denmark
   c. effects and healthy and diet and women and Nordic countries
   d. diet and (Sweden or Denmark) and (women or female)

4. A search of the UA library catalog (not Worldcat Local) will locate which types of materials?

   Question options:
   a. Full text of articles, images, and books
   b. Books, journals, and video recordings
   c. Articles, newspapers, and archives
   d. Popular articles, scholarly books, and web sites

5. In your search statement, you can place an asterisk (*) at the end of a keyword, for example, advertis*, to retrieve articles that have this root word
   and a variety of endings of this word. Which option below would work
   best for a search on a topic related to teenagers?

   Question options:
   a. Teens*
   b. Teenager*
   c. Teenagers*
   d. Teen*

6. What is one reason why a graduate student may want to use social media?
   Enter you answer below.

7. Select the correct response below to complete this sentence: The current
   U.S. copyright laws

   Question options:
   a. protect the ideas of authors.
   b. don't require the display of the copyright symbol.
   c. allow works published before 1928 to be in the public domain.
   d. apply only to ideas and works from 1977 forward.

8. Which of the following databases matches this description?

   *Provides access to more than 1,000 leading academic journals across the
   humanities, social sciences, and sciences from the first volume up to the
   latest five years.*

   Question options:
   a. Web of Science
   b. Periodical Archive Online
   c. JSTOR
   d. Academic Search Complete

APPENDIX 2

Resource 8.2
Research Portfolio Requirements

LIBR 696a Research Portfolio Requirements
The Research Portfolio is an online portfolio of information resources tailored to your research interests and identified during the course in the weekly modules.

Content
Your portfolio site must include the following categories/sections, organized on separate pages:
- Introduction
- Information resources
- Information policy scholarly networking
- Annotated bibliography
-

You may customize your LIBR 696 Research Portfolio to include other categories or types of information resources, but you must meet the basic requirements described below.

Introduction: Your biographical statement, including research interests/description of dissertation/thesis topic. (See Week 1.)

Information Resources: Library Databases and Core Journals. (See Weeks 4–6.)

List at least two disciplinary databases and two core journals that are relevant to your discipline/research topic. The core journals can be identified during your database searches as you begin to see the same journal titles show up in relevant search results or you may want to consult with your advisor.

For disciplinary databases, include the following information:
a. Title
b. Coverage (subject, types of publications, years, etc.) Note: It is acceptable to use the database descriptions from the UA library web site.
c. Notes on your experience using this resource, including any unique features or search tips, etc.

For core journals, include the following:

a.   Title
b.   Coverage (subject, years available, etc.)
c.   Comments on the journal's relevance or importance for your discipline

Note: Remember, you can add categories in this section for other relevant resources.

Information Policy: Scholarly Communication, Open Access, Copyright, and Fair Use. (See Weeks 7–8.)

List at least two journal articles, editorials or blog posts, and so on reflecting disciplinary perspectives on one or more of these information policy and ethics issues: scholarly communication, open access, copyright, or fair use.

For each resource:

a.   Give the bibliographic citation, including the URL if appropriate
b.   Give brief comments on the article and why it is interesting/important or useful to you

You should be able to find the articles/blogs through database searches or by browsing professional society web sites or journals. If you cannot find anything specific to your discipline, go up to a broader subject area. For example, botany (specific) can be broadened to biology, life sciences, or agriculture. Contact the instructor if you are unable to locate items for this section of the portfolio.

Scholarly Networking: (See Weeks 2, 4–6, and 9.)

List at least one item for each of the following three categories, including a brief summary of why the resource/person is important to your research, etc.:

1.   Important authors/researchers
2.   Professional societies/associations
3.   Scholarly or professional social media sites (Facebook pages, Twitter feeds, Pinterest sites, etc.)

Include URLs for the resources listed for #2 and #3 but also, if available, for individuals listed for #1.

Annotated Bibliography: For the bibliography, select at least ten citations for publications related to your graduate research topic that you found through the database searches in the assignments.

a.   Use a consistent citation style
   •   List the citation style you are using at the top of the bibliography.

b. Write a brief annotation for each article, commenting on its value to your research.

Web Portfolio Design/Layout

Themes: Choose a theme that is appropriate for your research portfolio. There is usually the capability to modify the theme color and fonts used in the theme. Keep it simple—and readable!

Layout/Organization: Create a separate page for each content category in your Research Portfolio. Please organize your pages in this same order:

- Introduction/bio statement [Note: This should be located on the site's Home Page.]
- Information resources
- Information policy
- Scholarly networking
- Annotated bibliography

Organization options:

- You may wish to organize content into subpages for easier reading. You will probably need to log in to your email.arizona.edu account to access these pages.

  See Sarah Whitehead's Research Portfolio (Fall 2012)/ Information Resources page: [https://sites.google.com/a/email.arizona.edu/sarah-v-whitehead/information-resources]
- Or use tables.

  See Sarah Whitehead's Research Portfolio (Fall 2012)/ Scholarly Networking page: https://sites.google.com/a/email.arizona.edu/sarah-v-whitehead/scholarly-networking

Graphics: You are encouraged to include a photo of yourself on the introductory page. Other graphics are okay as long as they don't distract from the content. Keep it simple and readable!

NOTES

1. J. A. Arter, "Using Assessment as a Tool for Learning," in *A Handbook for Student Performance in an Era of Restructuring*, ed. by R. A. Blum and J. A. Arter (Alexandria, VA: Association for Supervision and Curriculum Development, 1996), 1–6.

2. Anne Zald and Debra Gilchrist, "Instruction and Program Design through Assessment," in *Information Literacy Instruction Handbook*, ed. by Christopher N. Cox and Elizabeth Blakesley Lindsay (Chicago: Association of College and Research Libraries, 2008), 166.

3. Paul Black, "Formative and Summative Aspects of Assessment: Theoretical and Research Foundations in the Context of Pedagogy," in *SAGE Handbook of Research on Classroom Assessment*, ed. by James H. McMillan (Thousand Oaks, CA: SAGE Publications, Inc., 2013), 167–179.

4. Megan Oakleaf, "The Information Literacy Instruction Assessment Cycle: A Guide for Increasing Student Learning and Improving Librarian Instructional Skills," *Journal of Documentation* 65, no. 4 (2009): 540.

5. Joan R. Kaplowitz, *Transforming Information Literacy Instruction Using Learner-Centered Teaching* (New York: Neal-Shulman Publishers, 2012): 112.

6. W. James Popham, *Classroom Assessment: What Teachers Need to Know,* 6th ed. (Boston: Pearson, 2011), 157.

7. Megan Oakleaf, "Dangers and Opportunities: A Conceptual Map of Information Literacy Assessment Approaches," *portal: Libraries and the Academy* 8, no. 3 (2008): 235.

8. Yvonne Mery, Jill Newby, and Ke Peng, "Why One-Shot Information Literacy Sessions Are Not the Future of Instruction: A Case for Online Credit Courses," *College & Research Libraries* 73, no. 4 (2012): 366–377.

9. Robert L. Linn and Norman E. Gronlund, *Measurement and Assessment in Teaching,* 7th ed. (Upper Saddle River, NJ: Merrill, 1995).

10. For more information, see Robert L. Linn and Norman E. Gronlund, *Measurement and Assessment in Teaching*; Thomas M. Haladyna, *Developing and Validating Multiple-Choice Test Items* (Mahwah, NJ: L. Erlbaum Associates, 1999); Mary McDonald, *Systematic Assessment of Learning Outcomes: Developing Multiple-Choice Exams* (Boston: Jones and Bartlett Publishers, 2002).

11. Linn and Gronlund, *Measurement and Assessment in Teaching*, 173–198.

12. Ibid.

13. Ibid.

14. Zald and Gilchrist, "Instruction and Program Design through Assessment," 174.

15. Kaplowitz, *Transforming Information Literacy Instruction Using Learner-Centered Teachin*, 102.

16. Ibid.

17. Oakleaf, "Dangers and Opportunities: A Conceptual Map of Information Literacy Assessment Approaches," 243.

18. Celeste Fenton and Brenda Ward Watkins, *Fluency in Distance Learning* (Charlotte, NC: Information Age Publishing, Inc., 2010), 180.

19. Grant Wiggins and Jay McTighe, *Understanding by Design*, 2nd ed. (Alexandria, VA: Association for Supervision & Curriculum Development (ASCD), 2005), 181.

20. Celeste Fenton and Brenda Ward Watkins, *Fluency in Distance Learning*, 179.

21. Ibid., 180.

22. Wiggins and McTighe, *Understanding by Design*, 182.

23. Oakleaf, "Dangers and Opportunities," 247.

24. Megan Oakleaf, "Using Rubrics to Assess Information Literacy: An Examination of Methodology and Interrater Reliability," *Journal of the American Society for Information Science and Technology* 60, no. 5 (2009): 969–983; Megan Oakleaf, *Writing Rubrics Right: Avoiding Common Mistakes in Rubric Assessment* (2009); Wiggins and McTighe, *Understanding by Design*.

25. Oakleaf, *Writing Rubrics Right: Avoiding Common Mistakes in Rubric Assessment*, 2–3.

26. Ibid.

27. Wiggins and McTighe, *Understanding by Design*, 182.

28. Oakleaf, "Using Rubrics to Assess Information Literacy."

29. *Rubric Assessment of Information Literacy Skills (RAILS).* http://railsontrack.info/; Lorrie A. Knight, "Using Rubrics to Assess Information Literacy," *Reference Services Review* 34, no. 1 (2006): 43–55; Fenton and Watkins, *Fluency in Distance Learning*.

30. Fenton and Watkins, *Fluency in Distance Learning*, 207.

31. Ibid.

32. Oakleaf, "The Information Literacy Instruction Assessment Cycle," 540–541.

33. Barbara Gross Davis, *Tools for Teaching,* (San Francisco: Jossey-Bass, 1993), 301.

34. Newell Chiesl, "Pragmatic Methods to Reduce Dishonesty in Web-Based Courses," *Quarterly Review of Distance Education* 8, no. 3 (2007, Fall): 207.

35. Davis, *Tools for Teaching*, 304.

36. Ibid.

37. Susan Ko and Steve Rossen, *Teaching Online: A Practical Guide*, 2nd ed. (New York: Routledge, 2008), 60–61.

38. Chiesl, "Pragmatic Methods to Reduce Dishonesty in Web-Based Courses," 206.

39. Ko and Rossen, *Teaching Online: A Practical Guide*, 60–61.

40. D. Eplion and T. Keefe, "Best Practices for Preventing Cheating on On-line Exams," ed. by G. Richards, *Proceedings of World Conference on E-Learning in Corporate, Government, Healthcare, and Higher Education.* (Chesapeake, VA: AACE, 2005), 296–297.

41. See more details in Davis, *Tools for Teaching*, 397–398; Stephen L. Benton and William. E. Cashin, "Student Ratings of Teaching: A Summary of Research and Literature." (IDEA Paper No. 50, Center for Faculty Evaluation and Development, Kansas State University, Manhattan, KS, 2012).

42. Benton and Cashin, "Student Ratings of Teaching."

43. Davis, *Tools for Teaching*, 365.

44. Quality Matters Program. *Higher Ed Program > Rubrics*, available at https://www.qualitymatters.org/rubric, accessed on January 16, 2014.

Chapter Nine

New Models for Teaching and Learning

INTRODUCTION

We certainly do not have a crystal ball to predict the future. However, we can be certain that online courses will continue to grow for public and private K–16 educational institutions, for on-the-job training and certification, and for nontraditional students ranging from immigrants wanting to learn a new language to baby boomers interested in exploring courses they never had an opportunity to take the first time around. Although specific technologies, apps, and LMS platforms may drop in status as the latest hot new thing, networked-based education will continue to evolve with content and engagement that can only be dreamed of today in order to provide access to a greater number of people.

Although advances in technology have led to the flowering of online learning, what we want to focus on in this chapter is a continuation of the thread we have emphasized throughout this book; that is, the pedagogical best practices for promoting student information literacy competency in an online environment. Through that lens we will examine four emerging areas that we believe will impact online courses in the near future: massive open online courses (MOOCs); the use of badges as alternative credentialing for online learning; the growing interest in the flipped classroom; and the future of online learning via mobile devices and what that means for online courses.

MOOCS

What can MOOCs tell us about the future of online courses? Focusing on the pedagogical aspects of MOOCs, research studies and surveys to date show that MOOCs are employing effective pedagogy,[1] including delivery of content through short videos; testing for comprehension through automated quizzing functions; learner-centered activities, such as online discussion forums; peer and self-assessments and the use of peer-endorsed "student gurus"[2]; and online forums for topic discussions. Following is a closer look at pedagogical elements of a MOOC that may provide insights into the future of online courses, as well as questions for librarians to ponder as online courses evolve.

Massive: Opening up the online course to thousands of students brings up pedagogical considerations of student collaboration, interaction, and assessment.[3] These are not new issues in online learning. Instructional technologists think that innovation and experimentation with MOOCs will lead to new best practices for student interaction and collaboration, including self- and peer-assessments.[4] The wealth of data available on a student's progress and achievement in specific aspects of an online course can be used to pinpoint places where individual responses from the instructor or teaching assistants can be provided.

We know from the MOOC experience that a majority of students do not finish the course when it is not required, but we do not know exactly why. What is known is that students that do well in an online environment are more self-directed learners. It takes motivation to enroll in a course and to do the work when there are no grades attached. What types of motivation works for students in a large online course? We know that having interactions with the instructor and other students and engaging learning materials are motivating factors. How can an instructor provide this level of interaction in an online class of thousands? Certification and digital badges may be one answer that we explore in the next section.

Open: One of the signature features of a MOOC is open access to any and all students. This raises questions about the barriers we see in our own online courses that in the future may be ameliorated with technology fixes or changes in information policy, such as a more flexible use of copyrighted materials and better access for students with disabilities.

Should our online courses be offered to any and all students? This is a central question for our IL programs and gets at the heart of why we are offering online IL courses. Can libraries afford to develop and deliver MOOCs? This would certainly lead to greater collaboration and sharing of learning materials among academic libraries and consortia.

Online: In the future, students will need not only to be information fluent but will need to have a mastery of digital literacy skills to thrive in a MOOC world of enhanced learning opportunities for collaboration and innovative learning materials. Digital literacy skills include creating or remixing content to create new knowledge; working with others to solve problems; connecting with like-minded individuals within and beyond the course; and having the critical-thinking skills to evaluate authoritative sources beyond scholarly publications, such as found in tweets, Pinterest, SlideShare, or Facebook.[5]

Courses: MOOCs personify an ongoing issue for online courses, namely the sustainability of truly effective online courses, given the amount of time and staff resources needed.[6] This is an ongoing area of concern for academic libraries, and one that librarians will be grappling with well into the future.

Another consideration for instruction librarians is the place of our online IL courses in relation to the MOOCs being offered at our institutions. We can use our instructional design expertise to collaborate with MOOC instructors to include portions of our courses into the MOOC, or offer our IL courses in tandem.[7]

DIGITAL BADGES

As discussed in Chapter 5, digital badges are beginning to gain more popularity in higher education, and they have many pedagogical elements that will help to ensure their wider acceptance. Digital badges allow students to show instructors and potential employers competencies they have mastered that are not readily apparent on a traditional transcript. These skills may include technology skills, project management skills, and of course, IL skills. Instruction librarians have longed struggled to show how their teaching activities impact student success, and digital badges allow libraries to offer students a method for showing what they have learned through one-shot sessions, tutorials, and IL courses. In online IL courses, digital badges can be used to demonstrate skill mastery of specific databases, ACRL Information Literacy Competency Standards, or discipline-specific learning outcomes.

Despite their growing popularity, digital badges have yet to gain wide acceptance by students, higher education institutions, and employers. We are currently piloting the use of badges in our undergraduate course and have found them to be an excellent way to organize and manage content while also motivating students. However, we also found that few students were familiar with badges at the onset of the course and most were uncertain of how they would use them in the future. Digital badges have also been criticized for how they motivate students with an emphasis on collecting badges and not on gaining skills.[8] Additionally, digital badges still lack credibility and validity. What does having an IL badge from a particular library mean and does it have the same meaning if it is from another library? These are some of the issues that will need to be addressed if badges are to become commonplace on campuses and in our libraries.

THE FLIPPED CLASSROOM

The flipped classroom is perhaps the most effective model for online teaching because it has the ability to bring together the best of both the online and face-to-face environments. Although not a new model, the flipped classroom, where students view lectures and complete tutorials before attending class, is becoming more dynamic than ever before. In an IL course, students can access readings and tutorials, meet online for discussions, and take quizzes before a library session. This in turn allows librarians to maximize the face-to-face (or synchronous) time they have with students. In a flipped classroom the instructor can ensure that all students have completed the same content and can tailor sessions to the particular needs of that student group. We believe more and more online and face-to-face instructors will embrace this model and it will become the norm across college campuses.

MOBILE

Although, not so much a pedagogical consideration as a technological one, any discussion of the future of online instruction must include a mention of mobile devices. More and more students are moving away from the desktop and even the laptop and toward mobile devices including phones and tablets. For online instructors this means that students will expect to have 24/7 access to all of your course content and will contact you and expect a quick reply any time of the day. Students will also expect that all course content including the LMS and the tutorials will work on their mobile devices in the same manner as other content they access. For instruction librarians, the rise of mobile devices means that they will need to develop the skills to create mobile-friendly content including apps and tutorials.

THE NEW INSTRUCTION LIBRARIAN

In our first chapter, we advocated for online courses, and we discussed many reasons why libraries should consider offering IL courses for both undergraduate and graduate students. As we look to the future, we come back to this idea of why libraries should create and offer online courses. Each year librarians across library departments are asked to move further away from the traditional roles of librarianship and into new work that emphasizes digital skills and broader competencies in collaboration, communication, and innovation/entrepreneurship. For the instruction librarian, these new roles mean a new way of looking at how we teach IL skills because one-shot library sessions are ineffective and most often focused on how to access and use a few tools.

The persistent growth of online courses ensures that librarians will need to develop the skills necessary to become effective online teachers. Thus, the instruction librarian of the future will not only need to know how to teach information literacy skills effectively, but they will also need to know how to use different LMSs, how to engage students in synchronous and asynchronous online environments, and how to create a variety of dynamic, multimedia tutorials for different student and departmental needs. Creating online IL courses provides librarians with the most effective method of developing these skills and competencies while learning a variety of instructional technology tools. Online IL courses allow librarians to interact with students in much more intimate ways and experience firsthand what works and does not work in the online environment.

We see the instruction librarian of the future with specialized degrees in instructional design and educational technologies, in addition to their library degrees, and although there may not be as many of us with this expertise, we can be confident that we will be deeply engaged in teaching students how to learn and thrive in a digital world.

KNOW THIS . . .

- Experimentation with MOOCs will lead to new best practices for student interaction and collaboration.
- In the future, students will need not only to be information fluent but will need to have a mastery of digital literacy skills in order to thrive in a MOOC world.
- In online IL courses, digital badges can be used to demonstrate skill mastery of specific databases, ACRL Information Literacy Competency Standards, or discipline-specific learning outcomes.
- Digital badges have been criticized for how they motivate students with an emphasis on collecting badges and not on gaining skills.
- The rise of mobile devices means that librarians will need to develop skills to create mobile-friendly content including apps and tutorials.
- In a flipped classroom the instructor can ensure that all students have completed the same content and can tailor sessions to the particular needs of that student group.
- Creating online IL courses provides librarians with the most effective method of developing instructional design and technology skills and competencies.

NOTES

1. David George Glance, Martin Forsey, and Myles Riley, "The Pedagogical Foundations of Massive Open Online Courses," *First Monday*. May 6, 2013, available at http://firstmonday.org/ojs/index.php/fm/article/view/4350/3673, accessed January 16, 2014.

2. Larry Johnson et al., *NMC Horizon Report: 2013 Higher Education Edition* (Austin, Texas: The New Media Consortium, 2013), 13.

3. Ibid., 10.

4. ELI Educause, "7 Things You Should Know about MOOCs II." 2013, available at https://net.educause.edu/ir/library/pdf/ELI7097.pdf, accessed January 16, 2014.

5. Larry Johnson, et al., *NMC Horizon Report: 2013 Higher Education Edition.*

6. ELI Educause, "7 Things You Should Know about MOOCs II."

7. Sarah M. Pritchard, "MOOCs: An Opportunity for Innovation and Research," *portal: Libraries and the Academy* 13, no. 2 (2013): 127–129.

8. Mitchel Resnick, "Still a Badge Skeptic," *HASTAC*. Feb 27, 2012, available at http://www.hastac.org/blogs/mres/2012/02/27/still-badge-skeptic, accessed January 16, 2014.

Index

ACRL Information Literacy Standards, 33–35, 37, 80, 82
ACRL Instruction Section Teaching Methods Committee, 41
active learning, 104–105
ADDIE, 30. *See also* curriculum design
ALA Office for Intellectual Technology Policy (OITP), 98–99
Americans with Disabilities Act (ADA), 113, 116. *See also* Universal Design for Learning (UDL)
Armstrong, Anne-Marie, 59
assessment: assessment-for-learning, 145; Bloom's Taxonomy, *147*; cycle, 144; formative, 144–45; multiple-choice items, 146–50; objective, 145–51; peer, 156; performance, 151–55; portfolios, 69, 129, 132–33, 152–54, 156, 163–65; pre- and post-tests, 146; rubrics, 152–55; self, 156; summative, 145; tools, 150–51, 157
assignments: benefits, 122–23; best practices, 124–26; case-studies, 128; collaborative group work, 127–29; comparing sources, 135–37; critical thinking skills, 123–24; databases, identifying appropriate, 82; e-books, locating, 140; expectations, 54–55; keyword selection, 106; learner-centered, 126; Paper Trail Project, 124; peer review, 129; sample (graduate), 131–34; sample (undergraduate), 135–41; scaffolding, 127; sequential learning tasks, 125; social media and scholarly networking, 133–34; Web of Science, cited reference searching of, 151; Wikipedia, 91. *See also* learning activities; assessment: performance
asynchronous instruction, 8
authentic assessment. *See* assessment: performance
authentic audience, 91

Babson Survey Research Group, 2
badges, 90–91, 171. *See also* learning materials: games
Badke, William, 2–3
Becker, Angela, 59–60
Bell, Steven, 2–3
Blakesley, Elizabeth, 3
blended courses, 8
Bloom's Taxonomy: assignments, 125; Iowa State University Center for Excellence in Learning and Teaching, 39; student learning

outcomes, 39–40; multiple-choice
items, *147*. *See also* learning
outcomes
Burkhardt, Joanna, M., 3–4, 124

Calhoon, Sharon, 59–60
Carnegie Mellon University, Eberly
Center for Teaching Excellence and
Educational Innovation, 128
Chandler, Paul, 106
Chickering, Arthur W., 20–21
cheating, 156–57
Clark, Ruth C., 113–14
class size, 129
constructivist learning theory. *See*
learning theories
Copyright Law, U.S., 97–99
Cournoyer, Carina, 3–4
course development: approval process,
14; credit hours, 36–37; time
commitment, 22–23
course evaluation: instructor self
assessment, 159; peer review, 159–
60; student learning assessments,
158; surveys, 159; teacher course
evaluation (TCE), 158
course management system (CMS). *See*
learning management system (LMS)
course topics, 33–36; Academic Search
Complete, 140–41; analyzing
articles, 136–37; Boolean logic,
106; citation management, 36, 122;
Copyright Law and Fair Use, 83,
97–99; dissertations and theses,
131–33; evaluating information, 35;
formulating a research topic, 35,
123–24, 129–30; information policy,
82; library catalog, 138–39; literature
reviews, 80; plagiarism, 127; primary
and secondary sources, 110; search
strategies, 80–81, 106–107; web
resources, 35–36
Creative Commons, 98
credit courses: benefits of, 4–5;
perceptions of, 2–3

critical thinking skills, 123
curriculum design: ADDIE, 30;
backward design, 31–33; course
goals, 33; course topics, 33–36;
environmental scanning, 30–31;
needs assessment, 30–31; personas,
use of, 32; scope and sequence,
36–37; Universal Design for
Learning (UDL), 96–97

digital badges. *See* badges
discussions: best practices, 84–85;
prompts, 84
digital literacy skills, 170
distance learning, definition, 8

e-learning, definition, 8
*Encyclopedia of Educational
Psychology*, 8
engagement, 108–110
evaluation: teaching effectiveness, 157–
60. *See also* course evaluation

Faculty Self-Assessment for Online
Teaching, 22
Fair Use Doctrine, 97–99
Family Educational and Right to
Privacy Act (FERPA), 18
Fenton, Celeste, 127
Fister, Barbara, 121
Foundation for Critical Thinking, 123
fun theory, 108–109

Gamson, Zelda F., 20–21
Gilchrist, Debra, 144
grading: policies and schemes, 53–54
group projects. *See* assignments:
collaborative group work
Gronlund, Norman E., 147, 150
Guide on the Side. *See* Tutorials
Gunselman, Cheryl, 3

Holliday, Wendy, 121
Hrycaj, Paul, 34
hybrid courses. definition, 8

Information Search Process (ISP). *See* Kuhlthau's Information Search Process (ISP)
instructional design. *See* curriculum design
instructional designer, 15
instructor competencies, 19–22
instructor roles, 15–19
instructor workload. *See* time management
interactivity: retention and transfer of learning, 106. *See also* tutorials: interactivity

Kaplan, Matt, 49–50
Kaplowitz, Joan R., 126, 128, 151
Kinnie, Jim, 3–4
Ko, Susan, 129
Krathwohl, David R., 39
Kuhlthau's Information Search Process (ISP), 81

learning activities: active and passive, 104–*105*; discussions, 83–85. *See also* assignments learning materials: games
learning management systems (LMS): course home page, 92–95; definition, 9; Desire2Learn, 155; navigation, 92–95; quiz feature, 150–51; requirements, 25–26; rubric template, 153, 155; student performance reports, 155
learning materials: alignment with learning outcomes, 81–82; copyrighted materials, 97–99; games, 90–91; lecture capture, 87; lectures, 86–87; podcasts, 87–88; readings, 85–86; screencasts, 88; social media, 91–92; textbook selection, 41; videos, 89. *See also* badges; video games; tutorials
learning objects, 9
learning outcomes, 37–40, 105–106; sample (graduate), 44–47; sample (undergraduate), 42–44. *See also* Bloom's Taxonomy
learning styles, 82–83
learning theories: adult learning theory, 20; cognitive load theory, 112–15; constructivist learning theory, 80–81
lectures, 86–87
Linn, Robert L., 147, 150

MacDonald, Mary C., 124
marketing, 18–19, 23–25
Mayer, Richard E., 106, 112–14
McTighe, Jay, 153–55
mobile devices: development for, 117, 172
Moreno, Roxana, 112
MOOCs, 169–71
motivation, 6; extrinsic motivators, 84; intrinsic motivators, 84. *See also* fun theory
multimedia principles, 112–15

Nielsen, Jakob, 115

Oakleaf, Megan, 154–55
one-shot sessions, 79–80, 146, 173
online courses: benefits of, 4–5; challenges for students, 5–8; effectiveness of, 3–4; enrollment in, 2; perceptions of, 1–2
online instruction, definition, 8
online learning, definition, 8

Palloff, Rena M., 125
passive learning, 104–105
Pearson Learning Solutions, 92
performance assessment. *See* assessment: performance
plagiarism, 126–27
Pratt, Keith, 125
Prensky, Marc, 109
privacy issues, 92
problem-based scenarios. *See* tutorials
professional development, 27

Quality Matters (QM): course design, 26–27; rubrics, 81, 160

Rathemacher, Andree J., 124
RefWorks. *See* course topics: citation management
Richards, Sylvie L. F., 56
Rogers, Jim, 121
Rossen, Steve, 129
rubrics: analytic, 152–53; discussion posts, 85; holistic, 152, *154*; LMS template tool, *153*–55; writing, 154–55

Sinor, Jennifer, 49–50
software: Adobe Captive, 116; Articulate Storyline and Presenter, 116–17; Lectora, 116; rapid e-learning software, 115–17; Raptivity, 116; Respondus, 151; SafeAssign, 127
SoftChalk, 59; TurnitIn, 127
social media. *See* learning materials: social media
student feedback, 22–23
student learning outcomes. *See* learning outcomes
student progress report. *See* performance: student performance report
subject matter expert (SME), 15
syllabus: benefits, 49–50; development, 50–56; elements of, 51–55; interactive, 56–59, 95; sample (graduate), 68–74; sample (undergraduate), 61–68; standard policies, 55–56; statement on cheating, 157; student use of, 59–60; tone of, 50
synchronous: definition, 8; web conferencing, 89–90

teaching assistants, 19
teaching strategies: flipped classroom, 172; for undergraduates, 20–21; instructor-centered teaching, 104. *See also* learning theories
time management, 6, 22–23, 129–30
Tinti-Kane, Hester, 92
Training. *See* professional development

tutorials: authenticity, 110–12; engagement, 108–10; interactivity, 106–108; graphics, use of, 113–15; help, use of, 112; humor, use of, 109; game elements, 109; Guide on the Side, 111; characters, use of, 109–10; problem-based scenarios, 110; text, use of small chunks, 115; mobile, development for, 117. *See also* interactivity; multimedia principles; software: rapid e-learning software

Universal Design for Learning (UDL). *See* curriculum design
U.S. Department of Education, 3

video games, 108
Van Hoeck, Michele, 91

Watkins, Brenda Ward, 127
web accessibility evaluation tools, 96–97
Windham, Scott, 56
Wiggins, Grant, 153–55
Williams, Karen, xiii
Worcester Polytechnic Institute, 128; workload management. *See* time management

Zald, Anne, 144

About the Authors

Yvonne Mery is an associate librarian and instructional designer at the University of Arizona. She has coauthored several papers on the integration of information literacy in online classes and presented at numerous national conferences on best practices for online information literacy instruction.

Jill Newby is an associate librarian at the University of Arizona and has been teaching information literacy at academic libraries for more than twenty-five years.

CALIFORNIA COLLEGE OF THE ARTS

CAC 00 0149009 W

ZA
3075
.M47
2014

DATE DUE